ASPATORE
Executive Business Intelligence

About Aspatore
Executive Business Intelligence
www.Aspatore.com

Aspatore publishes only the biggest names in the business world, including C-level (CEO, CTO, CFO, COO, CMO, Partner) leaders from over half the world's 500 largest companies, and other leading executives. Aspatore publishes the Inside the Minds, Bigwig Briefs, Focusbook and Aspatore Business Review imprints in addition to other best-selling business books and journals. By focusing on publishing only the biggest-name executives, Aspatore provides readers with proven business intelligence from industry insiders, rather than relying on the knowledge of unknown authors and analysts. Aspatore focuses on publishing traditional print books, while our portfolio company, Corporate Book Agents, focuses on developing areas within the book-publishing world. Aspatore Books is committed to providing our readers, authors, bookstores, distributors and customers with the highest quality books, book-related services, and publishing execution available anywhere in the world.

The *Bigwig Briefs* Series
www.BigwigBriefs.com

Bigwig Briefs feature condensed business intelligence from industry insiders and are the best way for business professionals to stay on top of the most pressing issues. *Bigwig Briefs* feature knowledge excerpts from the best-selling business books published by Aspatore books, other leading business book publishers, and essays written by leading executives for inclusion in a particular brief. Each brief represents the best way for executives to comprehend the most important information on a given topic in the most time-efficient manner possible. *Bigwig Briefs* is also the first interactive book series for business professionals whereby individuals can submit excerpts (50 to 5,000 words) for upcoming briefs on a topic they are knowledgeable on. (Submissions must be accepted by our editorial review committee, and if the excerpt is accepted the person submitting it receives a free copy of the book.) *Bigwig Briefs* are revolutionizing the business book market by providing the highest quality content in the most condensed format possible for business book readers worldwide.

About Corporate Book Agents

Corporate Book Agents assists leading companies and select individuals with book writing, publisher negotiations, book publishing, book sponsorship, worldwide book promotion and generating a new revenue stream from publishing. Services also include white paper, briefing, research report, bulletin, newsletter and article writing, editing, marketing and distribution. The goal of Corporate Book Agents is to help our clients capture the attention of prospective customers, retain loyal clients and penetrate new target markets by sharing valuable information in publications and providing the highest quality content for readers worldwide. For more information please visit www.CorporateBookAgents.com or email jonp@corporatebookagents.com.

BIGWIG BRIEFS:
BECOME A CEO

*Leading CEOs Share Knowledge Excerpts on What It Takes to Get
There, Stay There, and Empower Those Who Work With You*

ASPATORE
Executive Business Intelligence

Published by Aspatore Books, Inc.
For information on bulk orders, sponsorship opportunities or any other questions please email store@aspatore.com. For corrections, company/title updates, comments or any other inquiries please email info@aspatore.com.

First Printing, 2002
10 9 8 7 6 5 4 3 2 1

ISBN 1-58762-069-3

Library of Congress Card Number: 2001119813

Edited by Krista Smith

Cover design by Rachel Kashon, Kara Yates, Ian Mazie

Material in this book is for educational purposes only. This book is sold with the understanding that neither any of the interviewees nor the publisher is engaged in rendering legal, accounting, investment, or any other professional service.

This book is printed on acid-free paper.

Special thanks also to: Ted Juliano, Tracy Carbone, and Rinad Beidas

The views expressed by the individuals in this book do not necessarily reflect the views shared by the companies they are employed by (or the companies mentioned in this book). The companies referenced may not be the same companies that the individuals continue to work for since the publication of this book.

BIGWIG BRIEFS:

BECOME A CEO

CONTENTS

BIGWIG BRIEFS:
BECOME A CEO

Randolph C. Blazer, KPMG Consulting, Inc., Chairman and Chief Executive Officer

Advice for Business and Leadership

Take care of your people. Develop them, nurture them, and move them forward, because their success is your success. I would say a great deal of my personal success has come because I've been able to pick, recruit, mentor, and turn over much of the business to some very bright people, some of whom are probably brighter than I am. These professionals are able to catapult the business forward. To the extent that you can do that, you are going to be better off, and you will have those people to turn to. You will help ensure your own and the future success of the business.

The best leaders anywhere, whether they're government officials, business leaders, or sports people, are those individuals who understand the importance of people. They are very fair in how they treat people and how they want their business to treat other businesses. It's not just person-to-person; it's organization-to-organization, too. Being fair-minded is very important. It drives your culture and your success.

John W. Loose, Corning, Inc., President and Chief Executive Officer

Building a Company to Last a Hundred Years

A successful employee has to be bright – has to have some good innate process skills and decision-making skills. Because Corning was a family-run company for many years, people are well grounded with their values, and their values are consistent with what this company stands for.

We look for a special kind of human being. Corning looks for people who are here for a solid, growing career. We look for leaders. We recognize that there are individual performers and there are leaders, and individual performers are just as valued. In fact, the patents on intellectual property come largely from individual performers – the underlying strength of the company.

One of the biggest responsibilities of a CEO is to make sure we have people in place who can lead this company into the future. With my staff, I spend a lot of time on career development. If we have 15 people in their 30s and 40s who we think can lead the company in the future, we decide what to do to help them develop in their careers.

As you can imagine, it is very gratifying to be the CEO of a 150-year-old company. More importantly, we are a 150-year-*young* company. How have we survived all this time?

I think, when we look back on our history, the answer is in our DNA. Corning is unique in that it is very comfortable with big technology bets, and it's also comfortable being patient with its money. We spent years perfecting optical fiber before we made any money. We had hundreds of millions of dollars in losses in the LCD (liquid crystal display) business before we made any money. We are very comfortable making these big home-run technical bets, and they are industry-changing bets. When I talk about telecommunications, one of our big ideas is that we think telephone networks are going to run on protons, not electrons. We believe LCD will replace the CRT (cathode ray tube), and we know how to do it. We are very comfortable in capital-intensive businesses, so a big capital-intensive factory development does not make us uneasy. The payoffs are huge when you have proprietary technologies that are game-changers.

But you have to be very rigorous. This is ongoing and is certainly part of my responsibility. You have to be rigorous about your portfolio and know when it's time to cut and run. In the 1960s, when I was coming into this company, 65 percent of the company was devoted to television. Color television was the hottest item in consumer products; color TVs were starting to get bigger, and to get into the bedroom – it was an unbelievable market. Profits were pouring in, and it was great. Today it is an asterisk, and we have methodically exited the television business. We've made a bet on television glass over in Korea with our joint venture there – Samsung Corning – but we have basically backed away and invested in other technologies, such as LCD and telecom. We invented the glass casing for the electric light bulb – and now we are basically out of the lighting business. Lighting was the business this company was founded on – the basis of the company 100 years ago – but we are out of it now.

As with most companies that have lasted 100 years, this company is continually transforming itself. We watch the life cycle of businesses very carefully; we believe in it. You make your money in the growth stage of the life cycle. When you start going over the top of the life cycle, and it's getting mature, profits start to shrink. Then you get into decline, and it's over. We work very hard to anticipate when products will start coming over the top and then make plans to move on and reinvest in other types of technologies.

Challenges and Choices for a CEO

Having grown up in all of our businesses and being from the operations side, one of my biggest challenges is being the CEO and not the COO.

The CEO role is fascinating. The early challenge for me was dealing with the investment community. I learned that you deal with the investment community as you deal with everyone else. You're open, you tell them what you can tell them, and you don't surprise them. It's the way you want to deal with anyone. Your integrity is the most important asset you have with the investment community; everything you do has to be oriented around protecting that asset.

Another challenge that I think probably all CEOs face is the touch of loneliness at the top. I think you just have to recognize that and know that the relationships you had in the past will be different when you become a CEO.

A challenge for me is that I, a fact-based kind of decision maker, can never get 100 percent of the facts. I once got some advice to take the 80 percent I can usually get, and go with my gut. It works. You'll be right 90 percent of the time, and with the other 10 percent, you won't gain much anyway.

The advice I usually give others is to relax. Normally, when people come into my office, they are keyed up about something or some crisis of the moment. I always try to tell them to slow down, and we'll just deal with it. What is the data? What are the facts? Let's not shoot any messengers. Let's choose to deal with the challenge objectively, not blame anybody, and just work our way through it.

Looking Into Leadership

Many qualities of leadership come naturally. In my own life, I was a leader on the playground, and I was a quarterback in college. I have always been very comfortable with leadership, and I do think there is some natural essence in leadership. But you can truly move forward as a leader by making yourself learn. I spend a lot of time on my own personal development. I am a great believer in the idea that we're always learning. I think that's important in all individuals.

You should never typecast anyone, and never say a person has leveled. Don't generalize about people. I find that people are remarkable; some are early bloomers and fade early, and some are late bloomers and blossom late. This was true for me: I was a very late bloomer. I was a sales guy for ten years, and people thought I would be a sales manager one day. I got some breaks, though, and blossomed late. I've learned never to typecast people and never to generalize about what a person can and cannot do. You must give everyone a chance to succeed, and, equally, a chance to fail.

I think many of the fundamentals of management will change in the future. The piece I see changing the most is the move of more organizations toward team leadership. More and more, you see executive teams at the top of the company, rather than the traditional hierarchical type of organization that was typical in the past. Leading a high-level executive team presents some of its own challenges because you are dealing with people who are accomplished and smart and who already have a track record. There are also different personality styles among the team members – another set of challenges for leadership.

Pamela McNamara, Arthur D. Little, Inc., Chief Executive Officer

Leadership and Management in Turbulent Times

We now live in a world where all times are turbulent. This is either the first great lesson of the 21st century or the last great lesson of the previous century. With the accelerating pace of economic, social, political, environmental, and technological developments in today's world, change has become the norm for all businesses. This, of course, presents a host of challenges and opportunities as we seek to understand the nature of emerging developments and how to either accommodate them or leverage them in an innovative fashion in the marketplace.

A few key elements, summarized below, can help a company maintain a steady course in the midst of the push and shove of today's competitive marketplace.

Leadership

In becoming a senior leader at ADL, it has been important for me to embrace the differences between management and management consulting. After all, running a company, even a consulting company, is not the same as running a consulting project. The skills and insights of consultants are complementary to those of the clients we serve. Consultants provide the knowledge and experience in management and technology required to help firms innovate, adapt to change, or anticipate change. This requires both broad and deep context in technological developments, industrial practice, company operations, local and national economies, and organizational change. Just as the best coaches in sports were not necessarily the best players, the best managers are not always the best management consultants.

Nonetheless, the lessons of consulting have much to bring to the task of leadership as we face the challenges and opportunities of a turbulent world. Applying our own insights and experience to ourselves, however, is easier said than done for organizations more accustomed to dispensing advice than receiving it. An overriding philosophy of mine is that a leader should be the servant to the organization as a whole. The leader should serve in such a manner that the group as a whole does better – advancing, achieving its goals, and promoting good organizational health and vibrancy.

As in other businesses, a leader of a consulting firm must have a vision, both personally and for the organization. You must be deliberate and effective in execution, and you must have strong people skills. You need to be good at both listening and building consensus as you're building a team. But you also have to recognize when decisions have to be made at the expense of consensus.

Shared Values

Successful teams go through the hard work of understanding the characteristics, qualities, and shared beliefs inherent in the work they are doing, and the goals they're striving to achieve. They agree on the roles, the expectations, the contributions of the team members, how they relate to each other, and how they participate as a team. And they have a common major goal or vision that will stretch their capabilities, and the flexibility to do what it takes, playing full out, to reach it.

ADL's shared values, which have emerged from our long history, include a genuine drive to innovate, a passion for excellence, a spirit of collegiality, and a commitment to integrity. These values have consistently formed the underpinnings of our approaches to the marketplace as they have evolved over time. More to the point, they have been vital to the company's success over the years, and they are a crucial part of what attracts and holds employees. The company has been able to preserve and institutionalize the core values that have sustained us through many changes and, indeed, have become part of the ADL brand.

Balancing Strengths

Smart organizations maintain a portfolio of clients and industries, so that at any given time there is a mix of industry sectors and client organizations that can help the firm through normal client business cycles. It is also useful to maintain a range of services, some of which may be more appropriate for helping a client through tighter times and some of which can help a company take advantage of better times.

Balancing strengths is inherently a dynamic process. Not only do businesses go through cycles, but the underlying technologies driving innovation spring up, mature, and fade away.

A balance of strengths is also crucial to the client relationship-building process, which remains important at all times, whether the company is doing well or tightening its belt, and whether we are engaged in a specific project or not. By keeping in touch with firms at all times, we can keep aware of the challenges they are facing and offer our assistance where our current or emerging capabilities overlap their needs.

Setting Business Goals

Goal setting is a constant iterative process. Setting goals for the company is an activity we periodically refresh through think sessions and work sessions with our top staff. We have brought in not only the top leadership team, but also the most provocative thinkers in the business as part of our periodic strategy, budget, and operations planning. We cascade these plans and goals through the business in a way that invites input and response, a process that enriches the vision and direction of the company. It also helps set the context for, and promote clearer understanding of, more specific goals, measurable objectives, and the metrics we use to track the business.

Communication

We constantly reinforce goals and objectives – and our values and accomplishments as well – in our communications to staff. The head of global communications for our company works very closely with me and with our business leaders to frame not only our internal communications to staff, but also our external communications, along the major dimensions of our business strategy, operations, and achievements. Ours is a people business, and we are constantly evolving, refreshing, and communicating our plans and seeking input from staff. Keeping open channels of communication, both formal and informal, is essential in a business that relies on the cooperation and participation of a network of partners and associates.

Taking Risks

Taking risks is the key to anticipating the future. Although it is essential to have dependable, healthy practices to count on, we must also take risks to push out ahead into new domains or growth areas. Some of these gambles will not pay off as well as others, if at all. But a considered strategy of risk taking can go a long way toward promoting long-term success.

Hiring is another form of risk taking. In hiring individuals, you are often looking for people who, given free rein, can go the extra mile in developing novel approaches to addressing client challenges. Similarly, it is important to maintain enough flexibility in a consulting organization to allow individuals to test new ideas, approaches, or markets. Such experimentation can pose risks, but it can also lead to greater job satisfaction for the innovators, better results for the clients, and new opportunities for the company.

Bruce Nelson, Office Depot, Chief Executive Officer and Chairman

Foundation of Trust

The most important foundation for anything, but especially a business, is a foundation of trust. This trust must translate itself later into confidence. Trust is being as open and forthright as possible and as truthful as possible in every situation. In my business I try to be direct, to hold confidences, and to have no hidden agendas. That is how I manage, and that is the basis on which I build business.

Dialogue is essential because it creates opportunities for disagreement – because of the responsibility to express different viewpoints blended with facts and opinions. Facts and opinions are important considerations in decision making. They combine with intuition to form the basis for all major decisions. Dialogue means there is room for healthy disagreement, not disagreement for disagreement's sake, but to reach a better decision. When the disagreement ends, there must be unanimity.

The process must be highly participative. I never make a key decision without input. Sometimes I want input to reinforce a decision already made, or to provide different ideas and viewpoints for discussion. I am pragmatic in that the end result should dictate the approach.

I have a philosophy about bottom lines and people: people should never be ignored. Sometimes decisions need to be made that put people ahead of profits. This might contradict what shareholders want, but creating loyalty and a friendly environment where the employees like to work is more important than the shareholders' views.

Employees must always know where they stand. A manager must be clear with expectations and tell people if they need to improve their performance. The challenge of executives is to keep in touch with those who do the work and who really understand what is happening in a business – the employees.

When assembling a team of employees, strive for an eclectic group. Not everyone should be the same, with the same background and education. An effective team must be diverse in every way, such as in age, gender, and race. This will complement the diversity of the management team that brings different business experiences and life experiences to the business. The management team must be diverse in its views to complement the employees' diversity.

Great leaders are not distinguished by sheer brilliance, but rather by the combination of reasonable intelligence with understanding and empathy for people and the human condition.

A team must strive to work in a synergistic way, so that the group effort is greater than the sum of the efforts of the individuals on the team. That is based, again, on the concept of trust, which inspires open dialogue among the members of a team. When the leader is the only one who brings out the issues, always having to criticize and commend, the team functions less effectively than it would if peers were to speak up. Teamwork is more effective when peers speak to peers.

I try to encourage relationships between my workers, professional and otherwise. They need to trust each other. There is always conflict; conflict must be addressed with dignity, with no hidden agendas. Different viewpoints must be aired in different ways. Some people express themselves more assertively, while others are better listeners.

Leaders must always listen and look for the subtleties. The obvious about a certain employee or situation is easy to see; what is underneath is often more important. Essentially, the "underneath" deals with cause and effect; often the effects are the issues.

Working in Harmony

Management and the employees in a business must work in harmony with each other, directly and forthrightly, toward mutual trust and dignity. Being part of a team means no exclusivity. There is no room for favoritism in a team. The team's concerns come before the concerns of individuals. As the owner of a business, I want my employees to speak loudly about the state of their units, but I also want to them to be able to step back and ask, "What is the best thing for the whole – not just the particular pieces?" Promoting such openness and honesty in dialogue requires employees who are empowered to act and speak on behalf of their beliefs.

Employees need to *be* empowered to *feel* empowered, as illustrated in the difference between entrepreneurs and corporations. An entrepreneurial spirit gives an individual the freedom to initiate, respond, and create. Entrepreneurs can be creative, responsive, and quick to adjust to change. I want my decision making to mirror this entrepreneurial spirit. It is essentially authority with limits. The limits are not the same for everyone because people have different abilities and experiences. I try to allow freedom within a defined set of boundaries. When an employee grows beyond the boundaries, I will expand the boundaries for that particular person accordingly. It's important to allow employees freedom in decision making, but not to the point of isolating them. Thus, empowered employees develop over time, through experience.

Recognition, rewards, and actions become the indicators of an empowered employee. Learning stems from mistakes, so the CEO needs to determine where it is safe for employees to make mistakes. Sponsoring empowered employees takes place in the subtle, day-to-day workings and letting the employees have the measured autonomy and freedom to make decisions that may differ from the decision I would make in the same situation.

To become a leader in more than title, a CEO must have an inner drive that comes from deep inside. It must be more inside than outside. Many people are motivated extrinsically – by a bonus check or a new car, for example. I think that to be a true leader, you must have intrinsic motivation. To be a really great leader, you must have an insatiable appetite for accomplishments and results. You must always want to improve. That is a motivation to grow, to learn, and to convert this growth into action.

Great leaders are able to judge, coach, evaluate, and teach others. Great leaders replicate themselves. They are great selectors of talent. They can grow talent, nurture it, and reap its benefits. Great leaders are great with people. Leaders must also understand fully what they are leading. Leaders need to have a fire in their belly, a burning passion for what they do, and the ability to do what they love.

Leadership has its costs. Not everyone likes a leader. That sounds easy to deal with, but it is hard to value respect more than someone's approval. Leading a large corporation means sacrificing weekends, relationships, and time. Everything has a cost.

Responsibilities of a CEO

The first and most constant responsibility faced by a CEO is to sell his or her vision for the company and the future of the company. This always varies according to audience.

Relating to Wall Street is a matter of personal involvement in investor conferences, in conversation with major shareholders, in approaching the market of institutions and preaching the vision as an ambassador, a visionary. It is telling all these people, in all these settings, why your business is a compelling place to invest. That is the hands-on, personal touch that is needed to convince.

Top leadership follows a similar approach when communicating within the company. It is easier for a CEO to have contact with two levels of the organization – the people who report directly and those who report directly to them. I know them and contact them often. I spend an enormous amount of time with them individually and in groups. This face time builds confidence and trust.

When elaborating on these principles for larger groups, we must use modern means – for example, I send videos out once a month to my 40,000 Office Depot employees. We require our managers to see me on video. These videos are memos from the CEO. On our web site is a link entitled "Ask Bruce." I do not personally respond to all questions, but many times I do. I read my own email and respond often. I send many emails.

I alert our employees to whatever our company does in the public eye, such as what we give to charity. The CEO must communicate well and often. Sometimes this necessitates saying the same thing over and over in different ways. When I became CEO, I developed a mantra that was simple and easy to remember: "I want Office Depot to be the most compelling place to work, shop, and invest." I used that mantra over and over. We use videos, face time, letters, and memos to tell people that there is a vision and that the leadership is open, willing to communicate, and trustworthy. This ultimately persuades them to buy into the vision. If they buy into the vision, their output will be enormous. It creates a synergistic energy – magic happens.

The Three Focuses of a CEO

The three main day-to-day focuses of a CEO are people, money, and customers. People are affected through human resources, money is managed through the CFO, and customers are managed through marketing. The CEO needs sufficient data about all three. I examine the data based on its type, particular to the situation.

When dealing with people, I look for loyalty, turnover rate, progression rates, diversity, promotions, litigation, and how the litigation is resolved. I read the annual surveys. I see how leaders are developing and whether they are developing others. I look at whether the bulk of the people resources are internal or external.

When dealing with cash, I look at the cash in the bank, the balance sheets – not all of them, but enough to get an insight. If more is needed, I look for more. Some numbers will raise a flag, and these numbers demand my attention. To me, a good CFO is like a giant flashlight on numbers, illuminating the dark corners.

When looking at customers, I look for new customer growth, customer complaints, customer trends, and why complaints end up on my desk without being stopped before they get to me. I look at response time. I look at 15 to 20 indices daily. Based on what I see or sense, I may take the data further.

There must be a blend in priority of people, money, and customers. Ideally, they complement each other.

In the next ten years, the claims on a CEO's time will grow more demanding. Externally, the shareholders will want more face time. If your business is part of a community, then it will be expected to be more civically active. If the company is a major employer, it must participate in political and social issues, such as educating children. The CEO is always pressed to join a board to help raise money for certain issues. Internally, people want more access to the CEO. The workforce changes. It is far different than it was, say, 15 years ago. Employees are not as loyal in that they demand more leadership and change.

There are many variables now that must be considered by a CEO running a business. In the future that number will only increase. CEOs in the future will deal with more complexities. There are social, economic, political, and international variables, and the CEO must understand all of these. Technology's effects on business are difficult to keep up with, and global communication makes more information available to more people. Then the CEO must distinguish between information and data. Computers can give me information, but I have to determine what information I need to manage. With more information, there is less time for the essentials.

You can overcome these challenges if you have an appetite to grow and convert learning into practice while focusing on results and accomplishments. On top of this, you must still balance short- and long-term results. Today there is more pressure for short-term gain rather than long-term development. That is a problem of the American free-enterprise system. Stockholders are becoming more and more demanding. Being a CEO means juggling time, complexity, and political, social, and economic issues, then integrating all these pieces, fitting them together as a whole.

Thomas J. Silveri, Drake Beam Morin, Chief Executive Officer and President

The People

In order to be successful, you need to have a broad experience base and strong interpersonal skills. You need a well-rounded individual who has the desire and the ability to communicate, to listen, and to react, and the ability to do that in a way that is driven by the best interest of the customer. I look for people who have a strong overall skill set around written or oral communication. I'm looking for people who want to do something different and provide change. Those people are motivated and therefore successful.

As a leader whose background is in the personal services sector, that's how I was brought up. I am not interested in sitting in on internal meetings, trying to move my career forward that way. I'd rather be out in front of the customer. I enjoy that, whether it's on a personal level, a customer relationship level, or an external practice development level, or whether it's a trade show or new business meeting. But you have to want to interrelate. It is your job "satisfier." If you don't want that interaction, then the consulting business is not for you. If you stay in the business without this ability to interrelate, and enjoy it, you'll have a rather limited role within the consulting organization. You need to have communication skills, whether oral or written, and an intense desire to help people look forward.

Personally, I accomplish a balance by rigorously maintaining two non-work facets of my life: I take time to get away from the business occasionally, and I work hard at balancing my business and family time. I like to take one week off every three months, where I can get away and sit and think and read. I put this week in my book and make sure my secretary doesn't fill that time slot. I need time outside of the day-to-day rush to think of where the business is going and where it can best be supported going forward. I would urge all employees to do something like that. Taking a day off here and there, or every Friday in the summer, will not be enough to get you to "see the forest through the trees." That's how I handle my long-term needs. For me, balance of life is important, and to give myself that extra time, I just go in very early in the morning. Sometimes I'm in my office by 6:30 a.m., and I get home late at night. I work on my emails at night. When I'm there, I'm there. But when I'm gone, I'm gone.

Gary L. Moulton, Glyphics Communications, Inc., Chief Executive Officer

The LIFE Method

The LIFE Method will help your organization build and sustain a team of "thinkers," which, in turn, will bring to your business the very thing for which the method is named – *life*. There are too many companies that, through poor leadership, build an environment that can literally drain the life out of its employees. By focusing on four areas, a leader can ensure that he or she is creating and supporting a working environment that breathes life into its employees. The four stages of the LIFE Method are:

- Leadership
- Information
- Follow-Up
- Execution

Just as a plant needs a specific environment to develop and grow – the right type of soil, light, water, temperature, and so on – so does the entrepreneurial company. The LIFE Method will help create the specific environment for entrepreneurial thinking within a business.

Leadership

Leadership is like the soil. If it is full of nutrients (motivation, creativity, integrity, and so forth), then it will support the continued growth and development necessary for the organization to blossom. If it is full of poisons (control, finger pointing, dictatorship, et cetera) nothing can or will grow. It all starts at the bottom.

I know what you are thinking: Don't you mean the top? No. Why?

True leaders are great supporters. They are motivators. An entrepreneurial environment requires great leadership. When you think of leadership, throw out the old mindset with a hierarchical pyramid with the executive at the top. *Invert that pyramid.*

Did you know that the majority of Abraham Lincoln's letters were signed "Your Obedient Servant"? He didn't sign them "Your Commander-in-Chief," nor did he sign as "Your President." This speaks volumes about the leadership style of one of the world's greatest leaders.

The number-one killer of the LIFE Method is ego. I call ego the morning glory of leadership. Once it has been introduced into your entrepreneurial environment, it can quickly spread, feeding off the nutrients needed for the more productive aspects of business to flourish, until it has suffocated everything in its path.

There is nothing wrong with taking pride in a job well done – in fact, you should promote team pride, because it leads to confidence. You want confident employees. But if that pride and confidence turn into ego, if someone becomes focused more on the "me" instead the team, then that pride has turned into arrogance. Contrary to popular belief, there is no such thing as an arrogant leader. There are only arrogant dictators.

I often hear people refer to "entrepreneurial management," but I believe it to be a contradiction in terms. Entrepreneurs think outside the box, while managers work within it. Entrepreneurs focus on breaking barriers and developing new methods, while managers protect barriers like a guard dog to ensure that only "approved" methods are applied.

I prefer the term "entrepreneurial leadership." This is something that promotes an environment built upon creativity and thinking – the two prettiest perennials that can grow in your entrepreneurial garden. An entrepreneurial leader will continue to push for better processes and methods and encourage thinking outside that box.

Information

You have probably heard the phrase "knowledge is power." This is especially true in the context of an entrepreneurial team. The team members have to know the whys, whats, wheres, and whens of each project. Unless you want a garden full of mushrooms, don't fill it full of manure and keep it in the dark, because nothing else will grow.

Information is like water, and, if you want life to continue, you must keep it flowing. Without it, just as a plant will wilt and ultimately die, so will your entrepreneurial team. You must keep the team informed by giving clear objectives from the start and continue that flow of information as each project develops.

Follow-Up

Follow-up is like the gardener, and the gardener's tools are the measurables established for each project.

When I was a kid, I had to weed our family garden. I hated it. At the same time, I knew that if the weeds went unchecked for any given period of time, they would take over and there would be no harvest.

Execute

This is where you reap what you sow. If you have been focused on life in your garden, then you can ensure a great harvest. If not, well, you reap what you sow.

LIFE Method: L is for Leadership

Entrepreneurial leadership – not management, but leadership – is the most important part of the LIFE Method. "Attitude reflects leadership," to quote a line from the movie *Remember the Titans*. There are a many traits that I respect about leaders. Foremost, I respect those with a passion for what they do. When you are around these kinds of people, their passion is contagious, and it helps you lift yourself to the next level. If you've been around people like this, then you know what I mean because you've benefited from it as well.

Another trait of a great leader is integrity. One person who exemplified both passion and integrity was Abraham Lincoln.

Numerous books have been published about his leadership abilities, and I highly recommend reading them all. He really cared about people and led by example, by making suggestions and telling stories. At the same time, he knew when to draw the line. If people wouldn't step up, then he had no problem taking the reins to get things done. Knowing just when that needs to be done can be challenging, but it's one of the great things about being an entrepreneurial leader.

I learned a great lesson about integrity and its worth from a stranger when I was about 19. I was in California serving in the military and had lost my wallet at the beach. About three days later, I got a phone call from a man who spoke only broken English. He told me his home address so I could come and pick up my wallet. He lived in a very rough, nearly impoverished area. There were kids everywhere running in the streets, and I couldn't imagine how the families were able to support them. I went up to the door and the man returned my wallet. I looked inside to find that everything was there – cash and credit cards, all there. I had about $80 in cash in my wallet, which could have really made a difference in his life, but he didn't take it. I tried to give him some money to thank him for returning my wallet – him speaking his broken English, me speaking what little Spanish I knew – and he wouldn't accept it.

The entire experience had a profound impact on my life. I had always been taught about honesty and integrity, but this was the first time I truly understood the meaning of the terms. How valuable is your integrity? Would you sell it for $80? $100? $100,000? How about $1 million? I think about that experience whenever my own integrity is on the line, and try to ensure that my own entrepreneurial leadership reflects lessons I've learned like this one.

On that note, leadership can be taught. It's not something that you have or you don't. To learn to be a strong leader requires self-evaluation. You need to be able to look at yourself and what you're doing. You need to be able to see where you have faults and take the necessary actions to improve. Strong leaders are not arrogant or egotistical, but they are willing to take charge and make things happen when the time is right. The whole purpose of life is to make yourself better today than you were yesterday. You need to maintain a constant progression. That does not mean, however, that you do everything yourself.

Entrepreneurial leadership means allowing people to do their jobs, not managing with an iron fist. The entrepreneurial leader outlines the objective, then steps aside and lets the employee get it done. This includes allowing employees to make mistakes. This is not always easy, but it's critical to the long-term success of your organization. There are plenty of times I've bitten my lip about a minor issue, but let things follow their course because the experience would help the employee learn how to understand the issue from all angles. As a result, if the same problem comes up again in the future, it will be handled even more efficiently. This also allows the entrepreneurial leader to learn each employee's talents, as well as offering the opportunity to recognize your people for their successes. Recognition is critical to continued achievement. The challenge in motivating people is figuring out what each person needs to get his or her motor running. Some people need to be whipped to get the most out of them; that may destroy others. That's the most important part of employee motivation, and motivation is key to getting your employees to think like entrepreneurs.

If you just stumbled while reading this, let me reiterate. Getting your employees to think like entrepreneurs is a *good thing*. The entrepreneurial leader does not have a monopoly on entrepreneurial thinking. However, the entrepreneur is key to getting employees to think like entrepreneurs. In this case, it *does* start at the top. As I've stated earlier, entrepreneurial leaders offer leadership, not management. You set objectives, and then back away. It's important to think through the entire process, and that needs to be conveyed to your employees. They need to look at a problem from A to Z, which means weighing the various and extended repercussions of their actions. Often, employees are not allowed the freedom to think, so all they do is follow directives. In that scenario, they're robots, not people, let alone entrepreneurial thinkers.

At the same time, finding and hiring entrepreneurial people can be a challenge. One key element I've found is a positive attitude. I have never met a single entrepreneurial thinker who did not have a positive outlook on life. Plain and simple, it's not hard to convince yourself to fail. When I'm hiring, I want people who look for things to succeed, not people who see only how things can fail. Just pay attention and you'll see what kind of people they are. What I notice most about people are their personalities and personal drive. I actually pay more attention to these things than their individual talents, because you can teach skills. It's not so easy to teach someone to have drive and maintain a good personal attitude. Once they're hired, you've got to create an environment where employees can thrive, without squashing the entrepreneurial spirit out of them.

That's not to say that entrepreneurial thinking is something you have or you don't. Just as with leadership and specific skills, entrepreneurial thinking *can* be taught. If I have employees I want to encourage to take the next step toward entrepreneurial thinking, I may give them assignments here and there to see how they carry them out. If they pick something up and run with it, then they fit the entrepreneurial mold. If they're unwilling to step out of their comfort zones, then they will probably never learn entrepreneurial thinking. Entrepreneurial thinking is teachable, but not all people are entrepreneurial, and the entrepreneur needs to accept that. Just pay attention and see how each employee responds. Hire and cultivate the right types of people and they can help you and each other grow and progress.

This may sound like common sense, but I've seen plenty of situations where executives surround themselves with people who just praise everything they do. When this happens, it's no longer about success; the focus of the entrepreneur has shifted to stroking his own ego. You don't want a "yes man," particularly when you're in creative mode. You want people to question everything when it's time to be creative. You want them to look at a problem from all angles. That's why I may not even attend meetings where employees are evaluating a specific problem because I want their true thoughts, not the ones they think I want to hear. However, when a decision is made, I expect the same employees to stand behind it and move forward.

This is an important distinction to make. When it's time to move forward, your organization must *make progress*. There is huge value in giving clear direction, and then letting your employee teams make decisions and take action. At smaller companies, decisions tend to roll up to the entrepreneur. The larger the company gets, however, the less feasible this becomes. The entrepreneur needs to hire good people, but also ensure that good procedures are in place, with plenty of checks and balances. With appropriate checks and balances, the employee can make a mistake, learn from it, and improve for the future, without costing the company too much time, money, or other resources. With good procedures in place, the entrepreneur can feel confident that the company is heading in the right direction as it grows, which will make it easier to step back and let his or her people do their jobs. This, in turn, helps the employees take on a sense of ownership in a project and loyalty to the organization.

In most cases, I think being an entrepreneurial thinker gives more of a sense of loyalty and ownership in a business. This can be a very positive thing. The exception is when people begin to feel that something would not happen without them. That's ego rearing its ugly head again.

Nothing happens because of a single person. Every business is made up of a team of people, and a true entrepreneur knows when to step aside. An entrepreneur is like a perfect Marine. He storms the beach, then moves on. If he stayed, he would just be in the way. Some entrepreneurs are great at storming the beach but can't step aside and let their people do what they were hired to do. That damages any sense of ownership the employee may have developed. Entrepreneurs are great at creating, but true entrepreneurs see the project through creation and then hand it off when the time is right.

It's not always easy. In fact, the worst part about being an entrepreneurial leader is that people are *always* looking to you for leadership – and everyone's human. Some days, you may just not feel like being in leadership mode. But you have to be.

To get around this type of block, I try to find a situation in which I have to take charge and take on a job, and force myself to get past it. In other words, I force myself to move into leadership mode. This is particularly important when things are not going well. It's easy to be a leader when things are good. When things are not going well it's hard to be the one in charge, but that's when it's most critical that you do your job and do it well.

LIFE Method: I is for Information

The I in the LIFE Method can be interpreted as standing for two things: *information* (both the gathering and the dissemination), which can then lead to *innovation*. This is not to say, however, that innovation only results from deluging your employees with information. In fact, doing so can have the opposite effect. You want people to be able to see things through, but too much information shared too soon can fuel a feeling that things never get done. I stated earlier that information is the water feeding your garden. Remember that too much water can also drown the very things you're trying to grow.

For example, there may be 500 things planned for implementation over the next five years. But, after two years, only two of the hundreds implemented may have had an impact that employees could perceive, because they don't understand the big picture. As a result, they arrive at the conclusion that the executives don't know what they're doing. Although your intentions were good to present the big picture at the beginning of a long campaign, it ended up having a detrimental effect on the company. In cases like this, the entire company may not need the whole story at the outset, but would be better served by receiving it piece by piece over time. You water a plant every few days. Giving it a year's worth of water all at once is just a flash flood.

At the same time, if things are not going as planned and you receive negative feedback, you need to acknowledge the intent behind it. If the employee went to the trouble of voicing his or her opinion, this shows that the person cares at some level. So acknowledging the employee's input will go a lot further than saying, "It's going to happen this way or not at all."

Acknowledging input like this leads to an environment that is open to the sharing of ideas.

Your job as the entrepreneur is to create the environment where people can ask for input and share their thoughts without fear of reproach or ridicule. If people ask for input, provide it, but be careful not to get into a situation in which someone will never make a decision without your input. I avoid this by asking questions to guide the employee toward a solution. I know it can be difficult, but saying that something is a foolish or a useless idea kills a person's incentive to try. Asking questions and guiding them toward a more effective solution teaches them to go through the same process next go-round without coming to me. Next time, they may bounce ideas off other managers or their coworkers rather than the entrepreneur, getting everyone more involved. More direct involvement then results in more personal vested interest. More vested interest in a company and its projects is a goal in itself. You want your employees to care. You want them to take initiative. Fostering these types of behavior should be part of a company's strategic plan.

True entrepreneurs look forward to strategic planning. It can be difficult and it requires discipline, but there are ways to develop the needed discipline. One way to look forward to strategic planning is to anticipate the opportunity to fix things that may not have been executed well in the past. Every strategic planning session should begin by looking at where you were and where your planning may have been off the mark. Then go into information-gathering mode, and don't underestimate how much time this might take. *Never assume anything.* You may learn that the realities of providing a product or service are very different for those in the trenches than at the conceptual level. You need that information so you don't move forward with a half-baked plan.

Gathering and understanding information is key to being an entrepreneur. If there were two golden rules for maintaining entrepreneurial thinking, I'd have to say they're as follows:

1) Don't be afraid to ask questions.

Many great things come from people questioning the way things are done. Why? How? Can't it be done better? It's not being difficult or abrasive; it's looking for ways to improve.

2) Be aware of the situation around you.

Look for or create a niche. I've had the opportunity in a short time to surround myself with some talented entrepreneurs. If there is one thing they all agree on, it is *find a niche and fill it.* Just pay attention and keep looking for opportunities.

Once the information is gathered, go into creative mode. This is where it gets to be fun, because you have the opportunity to turn a past shortcoming into a success story.

When entering the creative environment, I implement cross-functional teams, where the people hit a project from all angles. In the development stage, even negative people can help point out weaknesses in a project that others may overlook. When I assign teams, I make sure they understand the end goal. I appoint a chairperson for the team and ensure that the chairperson has an assistant or backup. I also require that every meeting have an agenda. The chairperson and his or her backup are critical because even in a team environment someone needs to be held responsible. I personally believe that people will grow and innovate naturally if you give them the room to do so. If they need help, you give them help, but you don't do the work for them. But the team does not need to hold the reins the whole rest of the way. When the project moves out of creative mode, the cross-functional team may do more harm than good. Once the creative stage is complete, the teams need to be more focused on that particular stage, such as development or financing or sales. You're simply not going to hit the mark 100 percent of the time, and with proper planning up front, your misses will be closer to the mark.

Information not only feeds your employees, but it feeds the entrepreneur. This is another trick that a few of my mentors taught me early on: *read, read, read.* A ton of reading helps me stay on top of my knowledge base, which helps me keep my edge. And most of my reading is not business-related materials. I like historical books about presidents, generals, and leaders, inspirational and self-help books, and of course newspapers and trade magazines. When choosing my reading material, I use a little trick that a close friend taught me. If the book doesn't require you to have a pen in hand (for underlining the important stuff), then the book probably isn't worth reading. I cannot emphasize enough the importance of positive input in your daily life. There are so many bad things going on in the world that I honestly can't see how people get through the day without seeking out some positive message. If you can make something this important to maintaining your sanity part of your personal work ethic, you're already a step ahead of the game.

Why? Because being positive is crucial to selling your vision. Being positive results from confidence. The best place to start building that confidence is to ensure that you understand the vision completely. If you don't understand it, then you can't sell it. People need to buy into your vision. Your personality can play a big part in this. Two of the most useful classes I took in college were public speaking and acting. They taught me how to deliver a message in a way that people would understand and feel on a personal level. For example, using a little humor to warm up the audience is something business people often overlook. It has its place in business, just as it does in life. You've got to be real. You've got to be. If you're not passionate, then you need to go into a different business where you can be passionate, because people will see through you if you fake it. People are smart. They'll know if you're not sold on it, which will make it next to impossible for you to sell it.

LIFE Method: F is for Follow-Up

I stated earlier that follow-up is where you weed your garden. It can be tedious and may not be the most fun part of the LIFE Method, but it's absolutely critical.

Ensure that the strategy is shared and communicated accurately. Also ensure that the phases of implementation can be measured. Business writer Barcy C. Fox said, "What gets measured gets done. What gets rewarded gets done repeatedly."

Establishing measurables for each project is critical to success. Unfortunately, I had to learn this the hard way. I know that on the surface you may think that every organization understands this simple technique, but the reality is just the opposite. Consultants around the world get paid a lot of money teaching companies this simple strategy: measure your successes and failures, and align them with your corporate strategy. You also need to create a reward system for individual and team performance. This does not necessarily have to be a financial reward. It can be simple recognition for a job well done. There are numerous studies that prove that people crave public recognition. It also never hurts to tie performance bonuses or other incentive programs to executing well.

Of course, having measurables in place to quantify success will help you see improvement and focus on execution. You need objectives at all levels – individual, team and corporate. You should first establish corporate objectives and expectations that fall within your corporate strategy. Then set objectives at the individual and team levels to outline how you will reach your strategic goals. You also re-evaluate your goals periodically to ensure that they remain in line, so you don't get off track.

So it follows that the measures attached to performance are truly quantifiable. There's nothing wrong with challenging people – in fact, I think people enjoy it – as long as the challenges are fair and the goals are understood. Assigning goals that employees are incapable of reaching will only serve to demoralize them, and nothing positive can come from it.

LIFE Method: E is for Execution

You reap what you sow. Just as a farmer receives satisfaction during a bountiful harvest, so should you when a plan is executed to perfection. Remember that great entrepreneurs measure success by continued improvement, not by financial accomplishments. To progress means to learn from each experience, whether it was a success or a failure.

I think it was Louis L'Amour who failed to get a book published *16 times* before his seventeenth was finally accepted. What lessons do you think he learned from each failure? Yet, because of his tenacity, he continued writing and making submissions to publishers – and look what he accomplished. Another lesson from this is that some failures are simply caused by bad timing. What do you think happened to those 16 unpublished manuscripts once Louis L'Amour became a published author?

Always realize that execution is a dynamic – not static – process. You may find that you move back and forth between follow-up and execution as you implement a project, learn that something needs to change, go back, make adjustments, and relaunch. It can happen 20 times. Or it may be a perfect plan, executed flawlessly, resulting in the birth of a new leader within your organization. These are the moments that make it all worth it.

The greatest reward a leader receives is to watch the progression of individuals as they blossom into great leaders themselves.

The way you can help is to be clear in what you expect, then back off and let your employees do their jobs. If you have set clear objectives, and if you offer them the support of a true leader, then they will find a way to accomplish these goals.

Conclusion

I do not recall where I heard it, but isn't it interesting that a six-foot-tall man can have all the agility in the world, while an eight-foot-tall man can barely move? It is the same in business: large companies have a tendency to be very lethargic. They get caught in the corporate web, where employees are simply faceless numbers. This is sad, because tapping into employee wisdom is one of the greatest assets a company has, yet so few take advantage of it.

Because of the rapid changes in technology, companies that think entrepreneurially will thrive, regardless of size. What's the big thing today won't be tomorrow. Entrepreneurial companies will make adjustments to shifts in the market, and make the necessary changes to accommodate new technologies and needs. Doing so will ensure that the company will survive and thrive.

The best entrepreneurs are those who can see a project from the 50,000-foot level. There are a lot of ideas in the world, but they get nowhere unless they are put on paper. Translating the idea onto paper forces the entrepreneur to think it through in detail; then he or she must communicate it well to the employees. I have met many people with amazing ideas, but who end up justifying why it's not the right time to move forward with them. This is sad. Justification is the great killer of entrepreneurialism. If you can think of one reason why something should not be done, look again and think of five more why it should.

Thomas C. Sullivan, RPM, Inc., Chief Executive Officer

Becoming a Business Leader

There is no set formula for becoming a leader in business. Different people lead in different ways. You have to be very comfortable in what you are doing, like what you're doing, have integrity, and work hard. I do think it's that simple. I was a B student, and I'm probably one of the few in my company without a master's degree. I nearly flunked chemistry. I wasn't the greatest student. After college, I was a communications officer aboard a destroyer in the Navy for a couple of years. At the tender age of 23, I had 60 men under me – some were kids, and others were older than I was. And I was told they were my responsibility. Every young person who wants to grow up to be a leader should have a similar experience. To know how to lead, you first have to learn how to follow. I think you have to understand that.

To keep a company moving in the right direction, we have offered and given tremendous autonomy to companies that we've acquired. You could be looking at 20 individual units, which are actually operating as part of one RPM in the coatings industry. Because we broke the larger entity into smaller units, it's much easier to manage its growth. Growing a $100 million company to $500 million in the next five years is much more meaningful than growing a $2 billion company to $5 billion over the same period. It's the way we have broken down our operations into smaller units and put each of those operations on annual planning. Although we look at stretch plans over a three- to five-year period, we have very good control over an annual plan, and that's essentially how we operate.

Management Basics

As CEO, my most important responsibility involves communicating our strategies both to our people and to the financial community. In addition, there's the responsibility to ensure that our operations take advantage of the synergies among them, since they're all essentially part of the same industry. Then, it's basically waving the flag.

To wave the flag at RPM, it is essential to focus on our two constituencies: our shareholders and our employees. After that, I then encourage our operating people to go out and serve their customers. I think it would be nearly impossible for RPM, Inc. to be customer intimate; so that's left to the various operational units. Obviously, we have to be conscious and aware of the needs of the major companies in the consumer area, principally the mass merchandisers.

To manage successfully through all sorts of turbulence in the economy, it is important that management doesn't swing and sway with what is happening to the economy. RPM has had 52 consecutive record years in sales and earnings. I became CEO in 1971, when we were an $11 million company. It grew from that point for 32 consecutive record-setting years in sales and earnings, and we managed through some severe raw-material shortages, the inflation of the 1980s, and about four major recessions, including the one we're in now. With the exception of the last two years, the results from that period were all good. In fact, we have now had 54 consecutive years with record-setting increases in revenues, and in all but one of those 54 years we increased earnings year after year.

We position our smaller units to thrive on change in the marketplace. RPM is not in the position to drive any of the operations. We provide them with incentives to do a good job.

When RPM, Inc. acquired Rust-Oleum in 1994, it was a specialized, small-package, rust-inhibitive coatings company that owned its market. One of its well-known competitors decided it would try to expand its market from the general and decorative small-package paints position and go after the rust inhibitor. They were advertising on TV, and my thought was, "Uh-oh. We may have acquired a company that that came with more competition than we expected." The people at the operating level – the Rust-Oleum people, not the RPM people – said the way to combat this was to go after the general and all-purpose market. Today, Rust-Oleum is more than three times the competitor's size and controls a good majority of the broader all-purpose, decorative, spray-in, small-package market. Basically, this success was achieved though category management, where the top people at the operating level made the adjustments and made a better situation out of adversity.

To plan, a CEO must try to set realistic goals. Back in the 1980s, we told everyone that we wanted to see their growth at double-digit levels. Back in the 1980s, we also had inflation that was 6 to 8 percent, so that goal was more meaningful. Inflation in the 1990s kept our internal growth somewhat below the mid-single digits. We told our operations they could get to double-digit growth with our help by adding product lines through acquisitions. We've been able to maintain that trend throughout the 1990s, even though there was no inflation during that period.

To set goals and put the company in an advantageous position to reach those goals, a CEO can look at the plan in two different ways. First, it is the CEO's responsibility to try to figure out where the company will be in five years. From 1971 to 2001, we were very accurate in plotting the goals of RPM, Inc. to essentially double ourselves every five years. Along with that, as CEO you have to figure out what you're going to need in that process in terms of corporate support, and what you're going to need at the operating level in terms of support. You then tell the operating people, "OK, keep this five-year goal in line, but we want to hear from you only on a 12- to 18-month plan. Give us something in 12 to 18 months that correlates to what we are doing, but something you can do." Then we give them strong incentives to make that happen.

And it has happened, for two reasons: We've picked only good companies to acquire from the start, and we've kept our promise to give autonomy to good management. We never felt we were smart enough to do turnarounds. So we've picked very good companies, some of which I had been following for up to 20 years before they joined RPM.

By putting the growth down into the smaller units, increasing sales annually on a continual basis doesn't look impossible.

Then, of course, growth also includes acquiring companies; acquisitions have accounted for about half of our growth over that 30-year period. So the combination of managing down – in the sense of having our smaller operations be a part of the growth-planning process – and making select acquisitions has proved successful for us in a consolidating industry.

Maintaining Your Edge

To stay current, I read when I can. More often than not, I count on my people. A little more than a year ago, they put a computer on my desk. My secretary of 40 years came in and said, "You press this button and it turns on." I email people back and forth, but I still get out of my desk and go talk to people. I think that's how you monitor the pulse of your business and motivate your people. They know you have a personal interest in them, and they know you're interested in having them do a good job, too. I think all of that gives people some confidence. You have to give people a pat on the back and say, "Good job." Sometimes that goes further than a pay increase.

You need a well of people to build a company that will last. Products will change a hundred years from now, and I wouldn't even attempt to guess what our products will be a hundred years from now. There may be substrates out there that don't need paint. I started in this business mixing chemicals in a drum with a wooden paddle. We've advanced greatly from there, but this isn't a high-tech industry.

The only area we've ventured into that was considered mechanically high-tech is rubber roofing. It became a commodity and was a huge mistake for RPM, Inc. We lost a lot of money, but we managed our losses and got out of it finally. We were one of the first into it with Gates Engineering. Then

Firestone decreed that it was rubber – it might be roofing, but it was rubber – and decided they were going to get into it. They took the price from 70 cents to 17 cents per square foot, and it ruined that business for us.

We've also gone through the e-commerce bit in the last couple of years. Our e-commerce department had as many as 14 people. We dismantled much of that, though, because we've found that we're not selling quite as much off the web as we thought we would. What the web has done for managing our systems and things of that nature is absolutely beautiful. We are doing a lot of architectural specs, but not much direct selling.

Keeping that well of good people relates to the founding philosophy my father had: Get good people, create the atmosphere to keep them, and let them do their jobs. We have used that as the driving philosophy for our growth, and we will continue to do so.

Justin Jaschke, Verio, Inc., CEO

The Power of Persuasion

To become a leader you need to have a firm grasp of the business and a framework for how the business fits together, and you must know the pieces that will make it successful. This provides organizational context for how you are trying to manage that business. A good leader has a grasp of what is possible and the ability to formulate a vision. You also need optimism that you can achieve your goals in spite of all odds. Some people say that to continue against long odds is unrealistic, but I believe a leader needs to be confident and optimistic to overcome the odds. As a leader, you must believe it can be done and must be convincing enough to get people to follow you.

That is another requirement of leadership – you must be convincing. You must be able to persuade people to follow you. You must be a salesperson at heart. You may not be on the front line selling a product, but you are certainly selling the vision and the opportunity. What impresses me most in other leaders is the ability to encapsulate a vision and make it compelling. One of the people I most admire is John F. Kennedy: He was able to convey a vision through his words, and he got people excited and enthusiastic about that vision.

Most successful leaders must have a strong element of persuasion to motivate and convince people that they should follow. In addition, you need a high tolerance for responsibility – you have to like it, in fact. You have to be the one who will make the final call when data and advice fall on both sides, and you must be prepared to take the blame when things don't go as planned.

Building a Hundred-Year Company

Building a company that will last a hundred years is a matter of going through the various phases and taking the appropriate steps in each one. In the early phases you are just trying to survive and initiate something that can grow. Then it is a matter of staying on top of it, growing it, and fueling it with the right amount of capital and people. Eventually it becomes a matter of institutionalizing it – the phase we are in now.

In the early days of building the company you are much more dependent on heroic acts of individuals to get there. As the company matures and grows, you have to move away from dependence on these acts to dependence on solid process and business discipline. You have to instill the kinds of long-term, sustainable processes that can be continued as people inevitably move in and out of the business and the company. It is a matter of having the right plans in place, both from a personnel standpoint and a business standpoint – understanding what is changing your environment and reacting to that. From a capital standpoint, you may realize that you need to become part of a bigger entity to survive.

One thing that strikes me, having been through different companies, is that they are amazingly resilient entities. It is actually pretty hard to kill a business once you get it to a certain size and scale. I have seen businesses go through enormous turmoil and change and still survive situations you would never have thought they could withstand. Part of that is getting the company to a certain critical mass and scale, and getting processes and business practices in place that enable a company's survival even as people change and the business evolves.

A key element in building a lasting company is managing risk. One way we have always approached risk management is to have multiple options. We have always tried to work multiple paths so we are not held captive to one solution or have only one alternative. Throughout our acquisition history, we have typically negotiated two or three potential acquisitions at once, so we were not forced to take on an acquisition at a price we did not find attractive, or we weren't left empty-handed. This has been the same practice as with partnerships. If you need a certain type of relationship to be successful, you want to pursue multiple paths simultaneously to get there. You deal with risk around choices you have to make. We try to do financial modeling and try to understand upsides and downsides, and understand the balance in the decisions we are making.

Another way you manage risk is by contingency planning. If things go wrong – and they can't always be perfect – you need to have a backup plan. The other important thing is to have a healthy debate and a variety of views. As mentioned before, my views tend to lean toward the optimistic side, and it is healthy to have more conservative and somewhat skeptical views on the table so we can consider all perspectives before making a decision.

Ultimately, there are three rules for building a company that will last. The paramount rule is "Don't run out of money." That is a piece of advice I first received when I decided to leave the consulting business early in my career and start my own business. The senior consulting partner sat me down when I was heading out the door and said, "I hate to lose you at this point, but as long as you are convinced you are going to go, the only advice I can offer is that once you start a business, it is a race against cash flow. You have to get the cash flow positive before you run out of money, and if you don't, the consequences are severe." That reality was present throughout my venture capital experience, where as soon as you complete one financing, you're into another to try to raise capital. You see it in this market, where you have an industry just littered with the bodies of companies that have run out of money. Many of them had good business plans, and even good execution; but a lot of them just got extended too far and were not ready for the downturn. So rule number one is "Don't run out of money."

The second rule is "Remember the importance of people." My own belief is that people are the most critical element, and it was probably best put by my former chairman, who liked to say,

"Nothing is impossible, as long as you don't have to do it yourself."

There is a third rule, which is a risk-management kind of mantra: "Run the business as if you are going to own it forever, or you probably will." You may eventually sell the company, but you should think as though none of those other things will happen. When you are running it as if you will own it forever, and the business is healthy and thriving, then a lot of other options, like potential acquirers or strategic partners, open up to you. But if you are assuming, or even relying on, those other avenues, you can find yourself in a real trap.

The Future of Management

As far as I can tell, the requirement to learn and adapt at an ever-increasing pace only continues to intensify. In that kind of environment, management will become less one-person-centric and more team-oriented. Because things move so fast and because there is so much information to grasp, it becomes more and more challenging for one person to do it all, and you will have to rely on a team. You will still have one person in the CEO position, but I think the burdens of that position will be spread more evenly across a broader management team in order to deal with the complexity and speed of change.

I think that leadership in the new economy will depend less on physical presence and more on virtual kinds of companies, and leaders will have to learn to be comfortable with a much broader array of communication vehicles – email, teleconferencing, and telephones, as well as in-person communication – because of the virtual nature of management.

I also think management will take an increasingly global perspective. The major trend in the world today is globalization – the breakdown of technological, capital, and market barriers, and the sharing of technology, capital, and knowledge across geographic boundaries. You'll therefore have to be much more comfortable dealing with diversity, dealing with different cultural nuances across the various parts of your company, and incorporating a broader range of management styles and approaches in order to be able to deal with globalization.

John C. McAuliffe, General Physics Corporation, President

Leadership

Intelligence is important for leaders. You have to get the right information and make prudent decisions. You have to have confidence when taking risks. You have to be willing to make tough decisions. Many leaders get into what's called "information gridlock," or they get into a situation where they have to make a tough decision and just can't bring themselves to make it. Leaders need the fortitude to make those decisions regularly.

Sometimes, even after gathering input from your associates and allowing people to have a voice in the process, your decision deviates from their recommendations. Honesty, openness, and communication are critical at this point. You have to explain to them why you're going to take the direction that you're going to take. It's tough to do, but a well-reasoned explanation goes a long way toward getting people on board.

The leadership model that GP tries to follow is that of "servant leadership," by which leaders are expected to do everything they can to ensure the success of their organization. This model was prompted by a corporate climate survey that was conducted to determine the effectiveness of existing leadership and teamwork practices. We actually turned the focus on ourselves, subjecting *our own* company to a very tough assessment.

The climate survey (needs assessment) identified specific shortcomings in leadership behaviors. A "leadership boot camp" was designed, developed, and rolled out immediately to address leadership training and development and teamwork. The battle cry of the boot camp was "Leadership and teamwork drive our performance." Once the top three tiers of corporate leadership had been trained, a second climate survey was administered; the results indicated dramatic positive change. What occurred was a dramatic and lasting culture change. GP now has a values-based, employee-driven environment in which every employee is welcomed as a business partner and a fellow steward, responsible and accountable for the company's success.

Sometimes leadership means taking a risk on someone, backing up an employee's new idea, or giving people the freedom to do their jobs in the way that suits them best. Great leaders earn the respect of their employees and provide an environment that fosters every individual's growth. Leaders must understand people and treat them right. If you do that, people will be willing to come under your leadership and support you when you need it. In the consulting business, if you don't treat people right, you're not in business – you're really nothing without your employees.

Richard B. Priory, Duke Energy Corporation, Chairman of the Board, President, and Chief Executive Officer

The Steady Pulse of Change

In today's business world, receptivity to change is a key imperative. The leaders in our company must possess both a mindset and a skill set that will enable them to anticipate and master change. Too often in the past, business professionals have viewed the ability to deal with change as a "coping" response. You weathered or endured change but certainly didn't invite it into your company or business environment! The healthier viewpoint, in my opinion, is to open the window wide and let the winds of change stir things up. Change is accelerating, it's transforming, and it's affecting every market we serve, every region on our map, every service we offer, and every one of us.

Change is an empowering force that has allowed my company and many others to grow in positive new directions. Over the past decade, the energy industry has evolved dramatically. Electric restructuring in the United State, privatization of international markets, the convergence of gas and power, and new technologies have all profoundly redefined our industry and outlook for the future. Those changes have been hard for some organizations to grapple with, and, as a result, we've seen our competitive field narrow as the strong and agile prevailed over the more narrowly focused. True to Darwin's theory, natural selection occurs in business as well as in nature. We've been fortunate in that we have a strong foundation and an ability to adapt quickly to changing environmental conditions.

I enjoy the constant pulse of change and the challenges and rich opportunities it brings. And I tend to surround myself with individuals who are likewise inspired and energized by the changing dimensions of our business environment. Our world is a complex kaleidoscope of shifting parts. Depending on your perspective, you see either advantage or chaos, opportunity or threat. And how you approach the lens is key to competitive success.

Change can be daunting at first, especially given the magnitude and pace that confronts us today. But business leaders need to become accomplished at managing the diversity of issues, problems, and challenges that come in the door. The leaders at Duke Energy must be able to manage change as adeptly as they manage people, projects, and financial results.

Ours is a competitive business, but competition, like change, is healthy. I enjoy competition and always have. From Little League to the board room and the golf course, I've found competition to be motivating, rewarding, and, at times, humbling. We tend to win our fair share, and we also lose some to worthy competitors. But both wins and losses should motivate your team – to either continue the streak or turn the tide. The win/loss cycle keeps you balanced. You pause – briefly! – to celebrate accomplishments and focus on the need to do better the next time around. Just when you think you have the competitive advantage, a good player comes along and knocks you down a peg or two. In the long view, those strong players who bring something new to the game do us a favor. Their performance makes us realize we have to get better – fast – and reclaim our competitive edge. Our company is full of competitive people who welcome the chance to test themselves and our strategy against the best, because they realize that going head-to-head with strong competitors ultimately makes us better and stronger.

Crossing the Bridge Between Planning and Results

Many people can craft elegant and lofty plans. But hammering out a growth strategy – translating directional words into actionable, tangible results – requires top-notch leadership and unparalleled ability to execute. Execution is the toughest part of the equation, but, in my mind, it is also the most defining and rewarding.

If planning is truly strategic, it involves spanning the expanse between where an organization is today and the shared vision of where it will be in the future. The strategic plan is a bridge between two points, one known and one anticipated. It links present state with future state and provides a platform from which a company moves forward.

Forward movement is a key point here because it is easy for an organization that has labored long and hard on a carefully crafted plan to stand forever at a bridge portal, admiring its design. We can become very enamored of our plans and the planning process, to the point that we lose sight of the destination.

Ultimately, you have to cross the bridge. You have to take the necessary leap of faith, believing strongly in both the validity of your plan and the vision of your future.

Having an idea is one thing. Making that idea a reality is another. In the words of Thomas Edison, "I have more respect for the fellow with a single idea who gets there than for a fellow with a thousand ideas who does nothing."

I constantly focus our team on driving and delivering results – real, quantifiable results. And I caution against declaring victory before we have fully executed our plan and achieved the outcome we sought. A natural human tendency is to coast a bit when the finish line is within view. But that sense of certainty and complacency can be dangerous. We don't count any eggs until the chickens are walking around.

Organizations must gain consensus and clarity about strategic objectives. You do that by communicating – continuously – your strategic objectives to business units, departments, teams, and individuals.

At Duke Energy, we expect every employee to be a strategist, to be able to make the link between his or her specific role and the attainment of our enterprise goals. That's critical to our success.

And if every employee is to be a strategist, the strategy must be clear, widely communicated, and practical and applicable to everyone's job. Employees must have the tools and abilities to make it happen. Duke Energy has a series of enterprise challenges associated with our strategic plan. One of those challenges, strengthening our team, is focused on ensuring that our team has the strategic skills, understanding, and ability to move us forward.

Building a Successful Team

Leadership talent is absolutely critical to a company's ability to effectively execute bold strategy and achieve strong results. Success requires a commitment to building bench strength throughout the enterprise – preparing employees and leaders to shape and succeed in the brave new worlds of our industry and markets.

Duke Energy is by no means alone in our quest to recruit, develop, and maintain the best talent on the market. In today's economy, we are seeing a real war for talent, and we know that to win in our competitive field, we have to win the talent war. We have to attract, retain, and develop diverse competencies and leadership abilities.

The winners in the war for talent will be those companies whose sense of mission is great and who view talent in the live-or-die mentality of battle. Top-tier talent isn't a war trophy. It's the most basic of business survival tools.

At Duke Energy, we are clearly defining the link between individual development and contribution to business strategy. We have processes in place for determining leadership developmental needs, creating developmental plans, and identifying the core competencies to which we aspire. Recognizing that intellectual capital is our greatest asset, we have fostered a learning environment that reaffirms our business strategies and motivates employees to take on more responsibility, assume more risk, and solve complex and demanding problems.

Leadership development is just good business. Investors consider the quality of a corporation's management. Talented people prefer to work for companies that invest in development. Customers prefer to work with corporations that can solve problems and add value.

Obviously, development is first and foremost the responsibility of the individual employee. An enterprise-wide leadership initiative by no means removes that individual accountability.

The corporation cannot substitute for individual attention, self-awareness, and dedication. But the corporation can and should champion a management focus on and support of development.

Infusing our employees with a clear corporate vision, with a shared commitment to continuous learning, and with competitive market, financial, and technical competencies is crucial to our success.

We need to provide an enterprise-wide knowledge base that facilitates the cross-business-line collaboration and integration that underpin our strategy. We need to be open to and on the lookout for rotational and cross-business-line development opportunities that add depth to our ranks.

Learning leadership occurs in many ways. In some cases it can be deliberate, intentional, and nurtured over a long cycle; other times it will be reactive and serendipitous. My goal is to increase the percentage that is deliberate, intentional, and planned – and that pays off rapidly – and to minimize the elements of risk, reaction, and mismatch.

Author and futurist Alvin Toffler wrote, "The illiterate of the 21st century will not be those who cannot read and write, but those who cannot learn, unlearn, and relearn."

Duke Energy is striving for leadership literacy, and we compete on brainpower, not brawn. Even though we're bigger than ever, our success will come from great minds working together to achieve great results. We need entrepreneurial, transformational leaders – leaders who have the foresight to make the deal, and the skills to make the deal work. Aire de Geus, head of planning for Royal Dutch/Shell once said, "The ability to learn faster than your competitors may be your only sustainable competitive advantage."

The word "career" comes from the French word *carriere,* which originally meant a "racing course." As a verb, it means "to move at full speed." In today's world, careers and leadership come down to a race against change. We are faced with growing as fast and as nimbly as the challenges we face in our work. The contest demands the best we have to offer personally and as a team.

We have very strong performers in our organization, who combine professional and business knowledge with commitment and enthusiasm. In our competitive environment, we need team members who come to work every morning with a spirit of constant, creative persistence. You can get knocked to your knees on some days, but you need to be able to stand up and get back in the game.

Management Style

I am extremely results-oriented, and characterize myself as a practical visionary. I have a clear view of a desired destination, and I am equally focused on the route we need to take to get there and the horsepower of our engine. I enjoy looking at strategies and focusing on the ones that will work, based on market understanding and shareholder value potential.

I'm also an integrator by nature. I tend to see patterns in data where others may see randomness, and I seek connections among our businesses, our people, our customers, and our markets. In a company as large and diverse as ours, building and maintaining the interconnections among business lines and geographic locations is challenging, but it's absolutely essential.

I also consider myself team-oriented. As my career has progressed, I've moved from the role of individual performer, which I thoroughly enjoyed, to marshalling and motivating team performance.

I have studied the science of applying resources wisely and leading teams to achieve desired results, and I find it immensely rewarding to focus our collective energies on achieving the highest level of performance and value creation. It is very satisfying to me when we reach the point where we have clear understanding, throughout the organization, of our goals and tactics; when employees understand their individual roles in company success and work together in new and value-adding ways; and when we execute a plan successfully, hitting the bull's eye on the target we've set. And, when the course of the arrow teaches us something in the process, that's the greatest reward of all. If the execution of one plan leads to bigger and bolder goals, and greater knowledge and finesse, then we have achieved success for the long term.

Frederic M. Poses, American Standard Companies, Inc., Chairman and Chief Executive Officer

Back to Basics

The business world's myopic infatuation with the "new economy" has cooled. The dot-com bubble has burst. The record ten-year expansion of the U.S. economy has officially ended, and the world economy entered 2002 in what was looking like a classic global recession, complicated by international tensions.

None of these conditions is welcome, but neither are they cause for panic. They amount to a reminder that economic cycles are still very much part of business life. Tough times also reinforce a valuable management lesson: Fundamentals never go out of style.

Consistent attention to the fundamentals of your business will help you minimize the damage in difficult economic times and make your company stronger and more competitive when the business cycle turns around. It's been my experience that managers who are on top of the fundamentals of their business are also on top of the shifting patterns in their industries. They are generally better able to anticipate changes in the marketplace, to "see around the corner," and to act with the speed and flexibility to take strategic advantage of what they see.

When I think about the fundamentals of a successful business, I have three major concerns:

People: Are we recruiting and retaining the best possible talent and giving our people maximum opportunity to develop and expand their skills and increase their value to the company?

Environment: Are we creating the kind of working environment where people are results-driven, where expectations are high, and where the organization is structured to help people achieve results?

Focus: When the economic cycle eventually turns down, do we keep our perspective and stay focused on the basics of growth building, such as improved customer service, competitive new products, and the kind of operating efficiency that supports profitability?

The People Factor

People are your pivot point. Any graduate business school program will emphasize the importance of strategic and operating plans. Those plans, though, are only as good as the people you select to implement them. Recruiting and keeping talented people is the real art of management. A successful company is built around people who can deliver and execute – people who understand a company's vision and can turn it into action that pleases customers, motivates co-workers, and creates value for shareowners.

You can't know with certainty what the company or the world will look like ten years – or even ten months – from now. Instead of relying on predictions, you have to rely on people in your organization with the talent to change the company as the world changes. Building a successful company requires people who are open to change, not just for the company but for themselves. Some very talented people will not survive organizational change because they themselves will not change. They are in yesterday's paradigm, which held them in good stead yesterday, but is a bad fit today and a disastrous career trap tomorrow.

Ultimately, business is a game in which you choose the best players and work the game plan or fundamentals to help them win. It's not a game of solitaire; it's a team sport. You have to give people the opportunity to get into the game and use both their technical and their interpersonal skills to make a difference.

It comes down to creating an open environment where people feel free to share and take risks, are encouraged to excel, and can expect to be rewarded for succeeding. That's a prerequisite for a good leader, and a priority for any CEO in identifying good leaders within a business.

Leadership takes passion, commitment, boldness, and self-confidence – qualities innate in leaders. You can build on and improve these qualities, but my feeling is that either people have them or they don't.

A real leader creates an open environment by being consistently open to the ideas of others. Nobody has an answer for every question or a solution to every problem. As CEO, I may be responsible for a decision, but I know my decision will be better if it reflects the best thinking of the right people in our organization.

I have probably learned more from people who have worked for me over the years than from my bosses. By nature I am an observer – a listener and a watcher. The idea is to learn from others, but not to impersonate them. As a leader, I have to learn from others and then connect what I've learned to my own passions and convictions.

Communication is a critical skill for a leader. You must communicate your vision, passion, and desire to win if you expect people to follow you. Your message must also be consistent. If your message today is "March north," and tomorrow it's "March east," after a while people will get confused and won't respond.

You need a vision you can articulate with consistency. Consistency has taken a bad rap as the "hobgoblin of little minds." In organizations, consistency is a welcome alternative to chaos. When leaders change within a business, a new leader might have a strong desire to make changes that are inconsistent with the role, strategy, or values that employees have been urged to accept in the past. If you have to break with the past, make sure people understand why. Without that kind of communication, they will understand only that their organization is without consistency, and it's a quick jump from there to feeling they lack leadership.

Communication also creates enthusiasm. It's a way to motivate and teach. For example, we write a letter once a month to our employees about some topic of common interest. It could be about speed or safety. It might encourage our employees to think about what they contribute to the company. We send out a letter quarterly on how we are doing financially, and we made a global satellite broadcast recently to employees in one of our divisions to talk about a transition we are making. You also can communicate by doing things as simple as walking the halls or walking the factory floor. Just imagine being able to talk to every employee every day in person to swap ideas and concerns. You would certainly have a better company.

It is rare that a manager builds a new team from the ground up, with entirely new players. You almost always start with some existing players who've been with the company for a significant amount of time, in some cases longer than their leader has. Chances are high that you have some substantial talent in this group of veteran players, and it's an important part of your team-building responsibility to recognize and develop the talent of these veterans. These people will bring vital continuity to your efforts if you also take on the challenging job of blending them effectively with the new talent you recruit to enhance or add skills and experience.

Assembling a great team, though, is just the beginning of your responsibility as their leader. Once you've identified your team, you have to make sure the members can work together and stay focused. The better the team is, the more motivation and support they need from their leader. To keep good people on a team, keep challenging them. As you retain your good people by giving them challenging and meaningful work, your team develops a reputation that will make it easier for you to recruit more good people in the future – so a virtuous circle is created.

Creating the Right Environment

There's an endless list of variables that can help create the environment that helps people excel, including a good cafeteria, a fitness center, an on-site daycare center, varied benefit choices, and a reward system that includes stock options. Beyond those tangible things, though, you have to create an environment that provides people with a framework in which they strive for success. A framework like that must include high expectations.

High expectations of achievement – for both individuals and groups – are essential to a thriving, growth-oriented organization. High expectations drive innovation, and innovation means change. If you have modest expectations, then your incentive is to work just a little harder to reach them. You won't change your fundamental approach very much because you'll probably ask the same questions of the same people and get the same answers and results. High expectations, by contrast, create an environment where people realize they can't get where they want to go by doing business in the same old way. That sets the stage for innovation.

It's been my experience that innovative ideas spring from interaction within small groups, rather than from an individual. To demonstrate, try a simple exercise. Write down your solution to a problem, and then brainstorm with your colleagues. I guarantee you will come out with a much better solution after conferring with them. High expectations bolster innovation and promote cooperation.

High expectations, translated into definable goals, also create their own discipline. They give people a framework for making decisions. If you have no idea of your leader's goals for the business, you have no basis for setting your own work priorities. You cannot be disciplined in what you do. Self-discipline occurs when people have a clear idea of what the leadership of the company expects from them.

It's also important to carefully target expectations and goals. If a company's leadership identifies 47 goals, an individual or team couldn't possibly develop the discipline to meet them all. But if people are asked to focus on three important goals, then they have the flexibility to move left or right, backward or forward, depending on opportunities. They can ask, "Which of these moves will get me to goal one, goal two, or goal three?" Given the right combination of clear expectations and operating freedom, people will be self-disciplined as they produce results.

Finally, it's important that employees have their own high expectations and set individual goals that align with those of the business. If employees appreciate and understand a company's expectations, they should develop their own expectations for helping the company achieve its goals. If you want them to set their expectations high, make it clear that the company understands and embraces the need for risk.

Risk taking is sometimes mistakenly viewed as taking part in something dangerous. To me, there's nothing more dangerous than trying to do things the same way year after year. Taking too few risks or none at all only creates a bigger risk that a competitor will beat you.

As a leader, you must see the value in trying new ways of doing things, support your team in their efforts, and accept that there will be wins and misses. Risk taking, by definition, comes without a guarantee. Your job, then, is to encourage risk taking while effectively managing risk. It's part of your responsibility in growing the business.

Managing risk is a skill you develop through experience. I've learned over time to focus on those projects or ideas that are risk-worthy. You can measure risk-worthiness by asking the classic question of whether the reward is worth the risk.

For example, I once worked for a company that created a stain-resistant carpet. At the time, the idea was risky because we didn't know if we had the technology to produce it, if we could get the customers, or if there would be a high degree of warranties involved. But the biggest risk was that no one had ever done it before. It was uncharted territory.

Yet we realized that if we succeeded, we could turn a commodity fiber into a branded fiber and sell it for a lot more money, making it a risk-worthy project. So we took risks. Would the innovation work? Could we market it? Would the customer pay for it? The product succeeded and more than vindicated our risk taking. It was a win, and everybody likes to win.

We did plenty of things that were risk-worthy but didn't win for us. So our approach to risk taking is like building a batting average and accepting that we will strike out now and then. Of course, a company cannot afford to undertake 20 high-risk projects at the same time because the likelihood of success is relatively low. It's important to maintain a balanced portfolio of high-, medium-, and low-risk ventures. Too many long shots with no returns waste precious resources.

When you choose to take a risk, you should evaluate that risk all. the time. Measure the odds every day, because they change, whether the risk is taken on a person, a new product, or a customer. Just because you took a risk and got on the road with it does not mean you should stay on that road. Sometimes you have to accelerate risk taking and other times you have to pull over and stop. Most people don't stop early enough when a risk begins to look bad. Hope is no substitute for reason. Unfortunately, people keep hoping for the outcome they want, even when the evidence tells them it won't happen.

Good companies take risks, but when the risk goes against them, they minimize their losses. It's like being a trader: Good traders play the upside and minimize the downside. They get out early enough to avoid a catastrophe. That's how you effectively manage risk, but it's a hard decision for a leader to make.

You will always have people who desperately want to move forward with a project. Their passions are engaged, and their rewards might depend on it. But sometimes a leader must say, "Enough is enough." Don't tell people they have failed, because failure creates an environment in which people are too afraid take risks again. You want to avoid that. Rather, a leader should help people understand that knowing when to "fold 'em" is an important part of managing risk.

When your company's leadership shares its vision with its employees, empowers them to act, and gives them the skills and tools they need, you create a formula to win. But you need to measure your progress against your goals, communicate your progress, and keep your employees focused on achieving those goals.

As a leader, you have the important responsibility of selecting the appropriate metrics. Any single metric in its own right doesn't give you an accurate measure of performance. You have to link metrics together. For example, you cannot look at sales growth without profit growth. Sales growth is an important measure of how well you are doing with customers, but it is not good enough. Or you can measure inventory turns, but you need to measure lead times, too. If you promise delivery in two weeks and then take four weeks, you're not doing a good job even though your inventory turns might be phenomenal. If you invest time in developing a meaningful measurement process for all major activities, it will pay off handsomely in increased efficiency.

As a starting point in analyzing your performance, look at your competitive position in your industry. If you are growing sales above and beyond others, it must mean you have the products, the marketing, and the service to be winning with customers – a good top-line indicator. Now, that top-line performance will be different in good versus bad times, but in any economic climate you can measure your success by measuring your top-line performance against that of your competitors. But don't fall into the trap of getting so enamored of your top-line performance that you neglect your bottom line.

If you have a lot of top-line growth and no bottom-line growth, you are just worshiping at the altar of market share without getting its rewards. Ask yourself, "Am I improving my fundamentals?" In a softening economy, you might not be making as much money as you were before, but if you are doing the fundamental things that make a good business, you will have progress to measure. Those fundamentals include buying better raw materials, producing better products with fewer defects and higher quality, and introducing new products. Don't make the mistake of easing up on measurements until the business climate improves.

At the American Standard Companies, we've made it clear that we have three constituencies: customers, employees, and shareholders. That's been our mantra from day one. We constantly ask what we are doing for those three groups.

It is easiest to communicate with shareholders. We set specific goals for growing our top line, our earnings, and our free cash flow. That is something our shareowners can understand. If we communicate it as our long-term goal, they can measure us each year. We believe that when we deliver on those goals, our shareholders will be rewarded with an increasing stock price.

For our customers, we simply ask ourselves, "Do we have the products? Do we have the services? Do we have the delivery time? Overall, are we becoming a more preferred supplier today than we were yesterday?" If the answer is "yes" to each of those questions, we'll see sales growth.

To our employees we owe opportunity. This means an opportunity to grow with the company, either by being promoted and having a different job, or by enhancing their ability to contribute more by learning and using new skills. We provide our people the opportunity to do that. It is their responsibility to take advantage of it. Those employees who take advantage will be more successful, have greater opportunity, and, in an uncertain world, have greater job security.

So I keep my eye on three things. First, I closely follow the pace of our business and how we are doing with customers. Second, I'm concerned with how well we manage talent. I ask, "Are we helping our people get better? Are we recruiting and retaining new talent?" And third, I keep my eye on our stock price. While on any given day our stock price is not a perfect barometer of how we are doing, in the long term it is an objective measurement of how many people want to buy our stock and how many people want to sell it. If we are doing a good job, then the demand will be higher than the supply, and the price will go up, so investors are the ultimate judge of our performance.

Staying Focused in Difficult Times

Difficult times don't mean you throw away your proven strategies and start casting around for miracle cures. In good times or bad, the fundamentals of the game do not change. You have a strategy, you have customers, and you have to execute.

It's always important to keep business cycles in perspective, but that's contrary to human nature. When the economy is good, people have a tendency to believe it will continue to get better indefinitely. When the economy looks grim, some of the same people convince themselves the situation will never turn around. So in tough times, you know pessimism will rise to the surface. You need to counter it with a vision that says, "We have good businesses. We have good people. We will do the right things. And the market and our business will turn around."

It's both motivating and reassuring for employees to hear that the best way to combat tough economic times is to dig in and work even harder on the same fundamentals we worked on in good times. Conditions might demand that we work a little differently. In difficult times, flexibility is your best defense against uncertainty. The market can slide away from you more quickly, so you want to react faster. And when the market picks up, you want to be the one who can take advantage first. So speed and flexibility are at a premium.

You can still make money in difficult times – in fact, you are paid to make money. Someone will sell products, and someone else will not. Our job is to be the one that sells – perhaps not as much as we would have sold before, but more than our competitors sell. Often that means creating new products that stimulate sales. You can also take advantage of weak supplier markets during difficult times to control your costs. For many companies, the toughest thing about tough times is realizing that you often have to work harder for smaller rewards. If you do that, though, you will be in a stronger position to grow faster than your competitors when the economy begins to improve.

There is always a weak competitor out there – someone who does not have the new products, the distribution, the cost structure, or the customer trust that they will make it through the difficult times. If you are a customer, you will go with the one you think will be there for you today and tomorrow.

It is interesting that bad economic times can also make you into a better business. When business is booming and your product lines are chronically sold out, you don't have the inventory or the motivation to create new products and services that sweeten your total offer to customers. But the improvements you make in bad times can significantly improve your fundamental position with customers and against competitors.

In good economies or bad, successful selling begins with understanding the fundamentals of your industry. The fundamentals of our industry say that many sales opportunities don't come around more than once. If I missed the sale today, I have missed the sale forever. If I miss the sale of a commercial air conditioning system today, I'm not going to recoup by selling two systems to the same customer tomorrow. It's a little bit like selling newspapers: If you don't buy today's newspaper from me, I can't make it up by selling you today's newspaper tomorrow.

Once you understand the fundamentals of your industry, you have to understand the timing of when your customer will come back. If an air conditioning unit breaks in the southwestern region of the U.S. in October, we know the customer might not replace it until March, when it starts to get warm. So that demand will come in six months. We have to be ready to sell when the customer is ready to buy, to understand his timing and be ready when he is.

Understanding the fundamentals, understanding your customers, and having the speed and flexibility to react truly distinguish companies that succeed in difficult times from those that miss the turn. They miss the turn on the way up because they don't understand the fundamentals of their own success. And they miss the turn on the way down because they don't understand the fundamentals of what's wrong with their business.

Keep Working the Fundamentals

Business fads come and go. Products and technology change. But the fundamentals of the game aren't all that different today than they were at the start of recorded commerce. In the year 2002, winning revolves around the fundamentals of finding customers, creating the value customers want, and delivering that value with enough efficiency to make money doing it. And I suspect things won't be very different when this new millennium comes to a close in another thousand years. That's why it's so important to have people in place who can change the company as the world changes.

ASPATORE
BUSINESS REVIEW
The Quarterly Management & Leadership Journal Featuring Exclusive Business Intelligence, Research & Analysis From Industry Insiders

Sample Contributors/Readers/Features:

John Zeglis (AT&T Wireless, CEO), Lawrence Rieger (Andersen, Global Managing Partner-Assurance Services), Richard Costello (GE, Brand Manager), Fred Round (Ernst & Young, Technology Tax Leader), Mark Fischer (Palmer & Dodge, Co-Chairperson IP Group), Steve Jones (Coca-Cola, Chief Marketing Officer), Warwick Ford (Verisign, CTO), Karen Edwards (Yahoo!, Brand Manager), Arnold Levine (Proskauer Rose, Chair, iPractice Group), Colin Cook (KPMG, Head of Transaction Services), John Hayes (American Express, EVP Marketing & Advertising), & More...

The Most Subscribed to Journal By C-Level Executives From the World's 100 Largest Companies

Aspatore Business Review brings you the most important, condensed business intelligence from industry insiders on a range of different topics affecting every executive, expanding your breadth of knowledge and enabling you to innovate and outperform.

Aspatore Business Review is the only way for business professionals to keep their edge and stay on top of the most pressing business issues. Each *Aspatore Business Review* features business intelligence, research and analysis from C-Level (CEO, CTO, CMO, CFO, Partner) executives, lawyers, consultants venture capitalists, investment bankers, and analysts from the world's largest and most prestigious companies. Each quarterly issue focuses on the most pressing business issues, trends, and emerging opportunities in the marketplace that affect every industry in some way or another. Every quarter, *Aspatore Business Review* focuses on topics that every business professional needs to be aware of such as:

- Staying Ahead of Changing Markets
- Profiting in a Recession/Market Upswing
- Emerging Market Opportunities
- New Legal Developments
- Investment Banking Perspectives
- Management and Leadership

- Fostering Innovation
- Brand Building
- Economy Trends
- Stock Market Outlook
- Technology and the Internet
- Venture Capital Perspectives

Aspatore Business Review is the one journal every business professional should read, and is the best way to maintain your edge and keep current with your business reading in the most time efficient manner possible.

To Order, Visit Us At www.Aspatore.com Or Call Toll Free 1-866-Aspatore (277-2867)

The Format of Aspatore Business Review

Aspatore Business Review is an interactive journal based on the submission of white papers, articles and knowledge excerpts from C-Level (CEO, CTO, CFO, CMO, Partner) executives from the world's top companies.

Each Aspatore Business Review follows the following special format, specifically designed by executives as the preferred way to comprehend business intelligence:

I. Executive Summary
The Executive Summary provides the highlight of the current journal, and enables you to very quickly scan the most important concepts.

II. ABR Feature
The ABR Feature focuses on a current topic affecting executives in every industry, from a variety of different C-Level (CEO, CFO, CTO, CFO, CMO, COO, Partner) perspectives.

III. In the Know
In the Know features knowledge excerpts from leading professionals on a variety of topics, enabling executives to expand their breadth of knowledge, communicate intelligently on a wide range of important issues, and develop ideas for innovation and new revenue opportunities within their own area of expertise.

IV. Industry Spotlight
The Industry Spotlight section highlights a current industry, or part of an industry, that is affecting the majority of businesses in some way or another and provides opportunities for growth and new profit centers.

V. Profession Spotlight
The Profession Spotlight focuses on a key C-Level (CEO, CFO, CTO, CFO, CMO, COO, Partner) or executive position, and the "Golden Rules" of that profession and other topics that will enable other types of executives to identify efficiencies, new product/service ideas, new revenue opportunities, interact better and implement innovative concepts into their own profession.

VI. Ideas for Innovation
Ideas for Innovation features brief one-line ideas for innovation from leading executives featured throughout the issue. The section also features a series of questions that can be used as a starting point for an executive meeting, brainstorming session, or distributed to key managers as a way to stimulate new ideas.

VII. What it Means
What it Means is a one-page summary by the editor of ABR, discussing the conclusions of the current journal and areas to watch going forward.

ASPATORE BUSINESS REVIEW-ORDER FORM

Call Us Toll Free at 1-866-Aspatore (277-2867)
Or Tear Out This Page and Mail or Fax To:
Aspatore Books, PO Box 883, Bedford, MA 01730
Or Fax To (617) 249-1970 (Preferred)

Name:

E-mail:

Shipping Address:

City: State: Zip:

Billing Address:

City: State: Zip:

Phone:

Please Circle the Journal (s) You Would like to Subscribe to:
Aspatore Business Review   Aspatore Entrepreneurial Review
Aspatore Marketing Review   Aspatore Technology Review
Aspatore Law Review   Aspatore Investing Review

Lock in at the Current Rates Today-Rates Increase Every Year
Please Check the Desired Length Subscription:
1 Year ($1,090) _____   2 Years (Save 10%-$1,962) _____
5 Years (Save 20%-$4,360) _____   10 Years (Save 30%-$7,630) _____
Lifetime Subscription ($24,980) _____

Number of Subscriptions _____   (3-4 subscriptions-10% discount, 5-10 subscriptions-15% discount, 11-20 subscriptions-20% discount, 21-50 subscriptions-30% discount, 51+ subscriptions-40% discount) If multiple year subscription is ordered, discount will be added to previous discount. If nothing is entered, we shall process the order for 1 subscription.

(If mailing in a check you can skip this section but please read fine print below and sign below)
Credit Card Type (Visa & Mastercard & Amex):

Credit Card Number:

Expiration Date:

Signature:

Would you like us to automatically bill your credit card at the end of your subscription so there is no discontinuity in service? (You can still cancel your subscription at any point before the renewal date.) Please circle: Yes   No

*(Please note the billing address much match the address on file with your credit card company exactly)

Terms & Conditions-We shall send a confirmation receipt to your e-mail address. If ordering from Massachusetts, please add 5% sales tax on the order (not including shipping and handling). If ordering from outside of the US, an additional $51.95 per year will be charged for shipping and handling costs. All issues are paperback and will be shipped as soon as they become available. Sorry, no returns, cancellations or refunds at any point unless automatic billing is selected, at which point you may cancel at any time before your subscription is renewed (no funds shall be returned however for the period currently subscribed to). Issues that are not already published will be shipped upon publication date. Publication dates are subject to delay-please allow 1-2 weeks for delivery of first issue. If a new issue is not coming out for another month, the issue from the previous quarter will be sent for the first issue.

To Order, Visit Us At www.Aspatore.com Or
Call Toll Free 1-866-Aspatore (277-2867)

BUILD YOUR OWN BUSINESS LIBRARY

Option A: Receive Every Book Published by Aspatore Books-Only $1,089 a Year- A Savings of Over 60% Off Retail prices

Receive every book published by Aspatore Books every year-between 60-100 books-a must have on bookshelves of every executive and an invaluable resource for quick access, business intelligence from industry insiders. Or send the collection as a gift to someone else!

The Aspatore Business Library Collection features must have business books on various positions, industries and topics, creating the ultimate business library for business professionals. The books in the collection feature business intelligence from C-Level executives (CEO, CTO, CFO, CMO, CFO, Partner) from the world's most respected companies, and represent an invaluable resource for quick access, business intelligence from industry insiders on a wide range of topics. Every business professional should have their own executive library, such as the top executives and great business leaders of our time have always had. The Aspatore Business Library Collection features the most exclusive, biggest name executives of our time and their most insightful words of wisdom, creating the ultimate executive library. Upon order being placed, you will immediately receive books published within the last month, and then for 11 months going forward (you also receive all titles 1-3 months before retail stores receive the new book). You may even request up to 10 books already published by Aspatore Books to be included.

Option B: 25 Best Selling Business Books-Only $399-A Savings of Over 45% Off Retail Prices!

Buy the top 25 best selling business titles published by Aspatore Books, a must have on bookshelves of every executive and an invaluable resource for quick access, business intelligence from industry insiders. Or send the collection as a gift to someone else! These books feature business intelligence from C-Level executives (CEO, CTO, CFO, CMO, CFO, Partner) from over half the world's 500 largest companies. Although every book may not be in your exact area of specialty, having these books on hand will time and again serve as incredible resources for you and everyone in your office. These books provide a wide array of information on various positions, industries and topics, creating a complete business library unto themselves. If you already have one or more of these books, please note this on the order form and different books will be added.

To Order, Visit Us At www.Aspatore.com Or Call Toll Free 1-866-Aspatore (277-2867)

Books Included:

Inside the Minds: The Wireless Industry-Industry Leaders Share Their Knowledge on the Future of the Wireless Revolution

Inside the Minds: Leading Consultants-Industry Leaders Share Their Knowledge on the Future of the Consulting Profession and Industry

Inside the Minds: Leading Deal Makers-Industry Leaders Share Their Knowledge on Negotiations, Leveraging Your Position and the Art of Deal Making

Inside the Minds: The Semiconductor Industry-Industry Leaders Share Their Knowledge on the Future of the Semiconductor Revolution

Inside the Minds: Leading Advertisers-Industry Leaders Share Their Knowledge on the Future of Advertising, Marketing and Building Successful Brands

Inside the Minds: Leading Accountants-Industry Leaders Share Their Knowledge on the Future of the Accounting Industry & Profession

Inside the Minds: The New Health Care Industry-Industry Leaders Share Their Knowledge on the Future of the Technology Charged Health Care Industry

Inside the Minds: Leading IP Lawyers-Leading IP Lawyers Share Their Knowledge on the Art & Science of Intellectual Property

Inside the Minds: Leading Labor Lawyers-Leading Labor Lawyers Share Their Knowledge on the Art & Science of Labor Law

Inside the Minds: Leading Litigators-Leading Litigators Share Their Knowledge on the Art & Science of Litigation

Inside the Minds: The Art of Public Relations-PR Visionaries Reveal the Secrets to Getting Noticed, Making a Name for Your Company, and Building a Brand Through Public Relations

Inside the Minds: Venture Capitalists-Inside the High Stakes and Fast Moving World of Venture Capital

Bigwig Briefs: Term Sheets & Valuations-An Inside Look at the Intricacies of Term Sheets & Valuations

Bigwig Briefs: Hunting Venture Capital-An Inside Look at the Basics of Venture Capital

Inside the Minds: Leading Wall St. Investors-Financial Gurus Reveal the Secrets to Picking a Winning Portfolio

Inside the Minds: Leading Marketers-Industry Leaders Share Their Knowledge on Building Successful Brands

Inside the Minds: Chief Technology Officers-Industry Experts Reveal the Secrets to Developing, Implementing, and Capitalizing on the Best Technologies in the World

Inside the Minds: Internet Bizdev-Industry Experts Reveal the Secrets to Inking Deals in the Internet Industry

Inside the Minds: The Entrepreneurial Problem Solver-Getting Yourself & Others to Think More Like an Entrepreneur

Inside the Minds: Internet Bigwigs-Internet CEOs and Research Analysts Forecast the Future of the Internet Economy

Inside the Minds: Leading CEOs-The Secrets to Management, Leadership & Profiting in Any Economy

Inside the Minds: Internet Marketing-Industry Experts Reveal the Secrets to Marketing, Advertising, and Building a Successful Brand on the Internet

Inside the Minds: Leading CTOs-Industry Leaders Share Their Knowledge on Harnessing and Developing the Best Technologies

Bigwig Briefs: Guerrilla Marketing-The Best of Guerrilla Marketing

Oh Behave! Reinforcing Successful Behaviors at Work With Consequences

BUILD YOUR OWN BUSINESS LIBRARY

Name:

E-mail:

Shipping Address:

City: State: Zip:

Billing Address:

City: State: Zip:

Phone:

Please Check Option A or Option B:

Option A _____ (Receive Every Book Published by Aspatore Books-$1,089 a Year)
Please indicate here any titles already published by Aspatore Books you would like in addition (there will be no charge for these titles as they will be included as part of the first month of books):

_____
_____
_____
_____

Option B _____ (25 Best Selling Business Books-$399)
Please indicate here any titles you already currently have (other best selling titles on a similar topic will then be added in their place):

_____
_____
_____

(If mailing in a check you can skip this section but please read fine print below and sign below)
Credit Card Type (Visa & Mastercard & Amex):

Credit Card Number:

Expiration Date:

Signature:

If option A is chosen, would you like us to automatically bill your credit card at the end of your subscription so there is no discontinuity in service? (You can still cancel your subscription at any point before the renewal date.) Please check: Yes _____   No _____

*(Please note the billing address much match the address on file with your credit card company exactly)

Terms & Conditions-We shall send a confirmation receipt to your e-mail address. If ordering from Massachusetts, please add 5% sales tax on the order (not including shipping and handling). If ordering from outside of the US, an additional $300 in shipping and handling costs will be charged for Option A and an additional $125 for Option B. All books are paperback and will be shipped as soon as they become available. Total number of books for Option A will vary from year to year, between 60-100 books. Sorry, no returns or refunds at any point unless automatic billing is selected, at which point you may cancel at any time before your subscription is renewed (no funds shall be returned however for the period currently subscribed to). Books that are not already published will be shipped upon publication date. Publication dates are subject to delay-please allow 1-2 weeks for delivery of first books. For the most up to date information on publication dates and availability please visit www.Aspatore.com.

To Order, Visit Us At www.Aspatore.com Or Call Toll Free 1-866-Aspatore (277-2867)

THE FOCUSBOOK™
ASSEMBLE YOUR OWN
BUSINESS BOOK™

Ever wish you could assemble your own business book, and even add your own thoughts in the book? Here is your chance to become the managing editor or your own book!

The Focusbook™ enables you to become the managing editor of your own book, by selecting individual chapters from the best selling business books published by Aspatore Books to assemble your own business book. A Focusbook™ can highlight a particular topic, industry, or area of expertise for yourself, your team, your course, or even your entire company. You can even add additional text of your own to the book, such as reference information, points to focus on, or even a course syllabus, in order to further customize it to better suit your needs. The Focusbook™ is the future of business books, allowing you to become the managing editor of your own business book, based on what you deem important, enabling yourself, and others to focus, innovate and outperform.

How It Works:
1. Select up to 10, 15, or 25 chapters from the choices on the following pages by checking the appropriate boxes. (Each Chapter Ranges From 15-40 Pages)
2. Decide if you want to include any of your own text to the book- maybe an introduction (as to why you chose these chapters), employee instructions (for new hires or to use as a management course/refresher), a course syllabus, information so it is applicable for clients/customers (reference), or even an article/white paper you already wrote. (Please note Aspatore Books will not edit the work, it is simply printed as is. Aspatore Books will not be considered the publisher of any additions and you will retain all rights to that content.)
3. Decide on a quantity.

To Order, Visit Us At <u>www.Aspatore.com</u> Or Call Toll Free 1-866-Aspatore (277-2867)

How the Book Will Look:
1. The book will be 5 inches tall and 8 inches wide (on the front and back). The width will vary depending on the amount of text. The book will look like a normal business book found in bookstores nationwide.

2. On the cover of the book, it will read "A Focusbook™ Assembled By," with your name on the next line (Jason Phillips in the example above). We can also add a company/university/course name if you so choose. Your name will also appear on the spine of the book. You can then also select a title for your Focusbook™ (such as Marketing Smarts as depicted in the picture above). On the back of the book will be the chapter names from your book.
3. The book will feature the standard Focusbook™ cover (see above), with the dominant colors being black with a red stripe across.
4. The chapters will be placed in a random order, unless a specific order is instructed on the order form. If you are adding your own text, it can be placed at the beginning or end of the text.
5. The book will feature the chapters you selected, plus any content of your own (optional), and a special section at the end for notes and ideas of your own to add as you read through and refer back to your Focusbook™.

Select the Chapters You Want on the Following Pages Then Fill Out the Order Form at the End

To Order, Visit Us At www.Aspatore.com Or Call Toll Free 1-866-Aspatore (277-2867)

Chapter #/Title	Author	Units
MARKETING/ADVERTISING/PR		
1. *Connecting With Consumer Needs	Stephen Jones (Coca-Cola, Chief Marketing Officer)	1
2. Staying Customer Focused	T. Michael Glenn (FedEx, EVP Market Development)	1
3. Building an Internet Mega-Brand	Karen Edwards (Yahoo!, VP, Brand Marketing)	1
4. Giving the Consumer a Seat at the Table	Michael Linton (Best Buy, SVP Marketing)	1
5. Building a Powerful Marketing Engine	Jody Bilney (Verizon, SVP Brand Management)	1
6. *Brands and Marketing: Evolving Together	John Hayes (American Express, EVP Brand Management)	1
7. Marlboro Friday: Branding a Product	Richard Rivers (Unilever, SVP)	1
8. Marketing Success: Providing Choice	Richard Costello (GE, Corporate Marketing Manager)	1
9. Turning a Brand Into a National Pastime	Tim Brosnan (Major League Baseball, EVP Business)	1
10. Advertisers' Conundrum–Change or Be Changed	M T Rainey (Young & Rubicam, Co-CEO)	1
11. *Rallying the Troops in Advertising	Eric Rosenkranz (Grey, CEO Asia Pacific)	1
12. Achieving Success as an Advertising Team	David Bell (Interpublic Group, Vice Chairman)	1
13. *Advertising: Invitation Only, No Regrets	Bob Brennan (Leo Burnett Worldwide, President)	1
14. *The Secret to Global Lovemark Brands	Tim Love (Saatchi & Saatchi, Managing Partner)	1
15. Soak it All In–The Secrets to Advertising Success	Paul Simons (Ogilvy Mather UK, CEO)	1
16. Likeable Advertising: Creative That Works	Alan Kalter (Doner, CEO)	1
17. Advertising Success: Tuning Into the Consumer	Alan Schultz (Valassis, CEO)	1
18. The Client Perspective in Advertising	Brendan Ryan (FCB Worldwide, CEO)	1
19. *Advertising Results in the Age of the Internet	David Kenny (Digitas, CEO)	1

* Denotes Best Selling Chapter

* Denotes Best Selling Chapter

Chapter #/Title	Author	Units
40. The Art of Public Relations	Dan Klores (Dan Klores Communications, President)	1
41. Passion and Precision in Communication	Raymond L. Kotcher (Ketchum, CEO)	1
42. Professionalism and Success in Public Relations	Victor Kamber (The Kamber Group, CEO)	1
43. A Balanced Internet Marketing Program	Meg Brossy (24/7 Media, Chief Marketing Officer)	1
44. *Internet Guerrilla Marketing on a Budget	Jay Levinson (Best-Selling Author)	1
45. Narrowcasting Through Email Marketing	Joe Payne (Microstrategy, Chief Marketing Officer)	1
46. Targeted Internet Marketing Strategies	John Ferber (Advertising.com, Founder)	1
47. Incentive Marketing on the Internet	Steve Parker (MyPoints, SVP Marketing)	1
48. B2B Internet Marketing	Tara Knowles (Viant, Chief Marketing Officer)	1
49. Breaking Through the Clutter on the Internet	Wenda Harris (Doubleclick, EVP General Network)	1
50. Measuring ROI Across Different Mediums	Mark Delvecchio (eWanted.com, VP Marketing)	1
51. *What is Guerrilla Marketing?	Jay Levinson (Best-Selling Author)	1
52. *What Makes a Guerrilla?	Jay Levinson (Best-Selling Author)	1
53. *Guerrilla Marketing: Attacking the Market	Jay Levinson (Best-Selling Author)	1
86. *Everyone is a Marketer	Jay Levinson (Best-Selling Author)	1
87. *Media Choices for the Guerrilla Marketer	Jay Levinson (Best-Selling Author)	1
88. *Technology and the Guerrilla Marketer	Jay Levinson (Best-Selling Author)	1
107. *Guerrilla Marketing on a Budget	Jay Levinson (Best-Selling Author)	1

CONSULTING/MANAGEMENT

54. *The Drive for Business Results	Frank Roney (IBM, General Manager)	1

* Denotes Best Selling Chapter

Chapter #/Title	Author	Units
55. *Understanding the Client	Randolph C. Blazer (KPMG Consulting, Inc., CEO)	1
56. *The Interface of Technology and Business	Pamela McNamara (Arthur D. Little, Inc., CEO)	1
57. *Elements of the Strategy Consulting Business	Dr. Chuck Lucier (Booz-Allan & Hamilton, SVP)	1
58. *Consulting: Figuring Out How to Do it Right	Dietmarr Osterman (A.T. Kearney, CEO)	1
195. Client Value in Consulting	Luther J. Nussbaum (First Consulting Group, CEO)	1
196. The Rules Have Changed in Consulting	John C. McAuliffe (General Physics Corporation, President)	1
197. Tailoring Solutions to Meet Client Needs	Thomas J. Silveri (Drake Beam Morin, CEO)	1
198. *The Future of Marketing Consulting	Davis Frigstad (Frost & Sullivan, Chairman)	1
69. *Fundamentals Never Go Out of Style	Fred Poses (American Standard, CEO)	1
70. High-Tech Company, High-Touch Values	John W. Loose (Corning, CEO)	1
71. Balancing Priorities for the Bottom Line	Bruce Nelson (Office Depot, Chairman)	1
72. *Keeping the Right People With Your Company	Thomas C. Sullivan (RPM, CEO)	1
73. *Gaining Entrepreneurial Momentum	Myron P. Shevell (New England Motor Freight, CEO)	1
74. Creating a Culture That Ensures Success	Justin Jaschke (Verio, CEO)	1
59. *Setting and Achieving Goals (For Women)	Jennifer Openshaw (Women's Financial Network)	1
60. The Path to Success (For Women)	Tiffany Bass Bukow (MsMoney, Founder and CEO)	2
61. Becoming a Leader (For Women)	Patricia Dunn (Barclays Global Investors, CEO)	1
62. Career Transitions (For Women)	Vivian Banta (Prudential Financial, CEO)	1
63. Making the Most of Your Time (For Women)	Kerri Lee Sinclair (AgentArts, Managing Director)	1
64. Follow Your Dreams (For Women)	Kim Fischer (AudioBasket, Co-Founder and CEO)	1
65. Keep Learning (For Women)	Krishna Subramanian (Kovair, CEO)	1

* Denotes Best Selling Chapter

Chapter #/Title	Author	Units
66. Keep Perspective (For Women)	Mona Lisa Wallace (RealEco.com, CEO)	1
67. Experiment With Different Things (For Women)	Emily Hofstetter (SiliconSalley.com, CEO)	1
68. Do What You Enjoy (For Women)	Lisa Henderson (LevelEdge, Founder and CEO)	1

LAW

Chapter #/Title	Author	Units
75. *Navigating Labor Law	Charles Birenbaum (Thelan Reid & Priest, Labor Chair)	1
76. The Makings of a Great Labor Lawyer	Gary Klotz (Butzel Long, Labor Chair)	1
77. The Complexity of Labor Law	Michael Reynvaan (Perkins Coie, Labor Chair)	1
78. *Labor Lawyer Code: Integrity and Honesty	Max Brittain, Jr. (Schiff Hardin & Waite, Labor Chair)	1
89. The Litigator: Advocate and Counselor	Rob Johnson (Sonnenschein Nath, Litigation Chair)	1
90. *The Key to Success in Litigation: Empathy	John Strauch (Jones, Day, Reavis & Pogue, Litigation Chair)	1
91. *Major Corporate and Commercial Litigation	Jeffrey Barist (Milbank, Tweed, Hadley, Litigation Chair)	1
92. Keys to Success as a Litigator	Martin Flumenbaum (Paul, Weiss, Rifkind, Litigation Chair)	1
93. *Deciding When to Go to Trial	Martin Lueck (Robins, Kaplan, Miller, Litigation Chair)	1
94. Credibility and Persuasiveness in Litigation	Michael Feldberg (Schulte Roth & Zabel, Litigation Chair)	1
95. *Litigation Challenges in the 21st Century	Thomas Kilbane (Squire, Sanders, Dempsey, Litigation Chair)	1
96. *Keeping it Simple	Evan R. Chesler (Cravath, Swaine & Moore, Litigation Chair)	1
97. Assessing Risk Through Preparation & Honesty	Harvey Kurzweil (Dewey Ballantine, Litigation Chair)	1
98. The Essence of Success: Solving the Problem	James W. Quinn (Weil, Gotshal & Manges, Litigation Chair)	1
99. The Performance Aspect of Litigation	Charles E. Koob (Simpson Thacher Bartlett, Litigation Chair)	1
100. *The Future of IP: Intellectual Asset Mngmnt.	Richard S. Florsheim (Foley & Lardner, IP Chair)	1

* Denotes Best Selling Chapter

Chapter #/Title	Author	Units
101. The Balancing of Art & Science in IP Law	Victor M. Wigman (Blank Rome, IP Chair)	1
102. *Policing a Trademark	Paula J. Krasny (Baker & McKenzie, IP Chair)	1
103. Credibility & Candor: Must Have Skills	Brandon Baum (Cooley Godward, IP Litigation Chair)	1
104. The Art & Science of Patent Law	Stuart Lubitz (Hogan & Hartson, Partner)	1
105. Successful IP Litigation	Cecilia Gonzalez (Howrey Simon Arnold & White, IP Chair)	1
106. Achieving Recognized Value in Ideas	Dean Russell (Kilpatrick Stockton, IP Chair)	1
108. Keeping Current W/ Rapidly Changing Times	Bruce Keller (Debevoise & Plimpton, IP Litigation Chair)	1
109. *Maximizing the Value of an IP Portfolio	Roger Maxwell (Jenkins & Gilchrist, IP Chair)	2
110. *The Power of Experience in Deal Making	Joseph Hoffman (Arter & Hadden, Corporate/Securities Chair)	1
111. *The Deal: The Beginning Rather than the End	Mark Macenka (Testa, Hurwitz & Thibeault, Business Chair)	1
112. Communicating With Clients	Gerard S. DiFiore (Reed Smith, Corporate/Securities Chair)	1
113. Making a Deal Work	Kenneth S. Bezozo, (Haynes and Boone, Business Chair)	1
114. Challenges for Internet & Tech. Companies	Carl Cohen (Buchanan Ingersoll, Technology Chair)	1
115. The Copyright Revolution	Mark Fischer (Palmer & Dodge, Internet/E-Commerce Chair)	1
116. Privacy Rights and Ownership of Content	Brian Vandenberg (uBid.com, General Counsel)	1
117. Business Intelligence From Day One	Mark I. Gruhin (Schmeltzer, Aptaker and Shepard, , Partner)	1
118. Legal Rules for Internet Companies	Arnold Levine (Proskauer Rose LLP, Chair, iPractice Group)	1
119. Protecting Your Assets	Gordon Caplan (Mintz Levin PC)	1
120. The Golden Rules of Raising Capital	James Hutchinson (Hogan & Hartson LLP)	1
121. Identifying the Right Legal Challenges	John Igeo (Encore Development, General Counsel)	1
122. The Importance of Patents	Richard Turner (Sughrue, Mion, Senior Counsel)	1

* Denotes Best Selling Chapter

Chapter #	Title	Author	Units
79.	*Common Values in Employment Law	Columbus Gangemi, Jr. (Winston & Strawn, Labor Chair)	1
80.	Building Long Term Relationships with Clients	Fred Alvarez (Wilson Sonsini, Labor Chair)	1
81.	*Becoming Part of the Client's Success	Brian Gold (Sidley Austin Brown & Wood, Labor Chair)	1
82.	*Understanding Multiple Audiences	Raymond Wheeler (Morrison & Foerster, Labor Chair)	1
83.	Employment Lawyer: Advisor and Advocate	Judith Langevin (Gray, Plant, Mooty & Bennett, Labor Chair)	1
84.	*Bringing Added Value to the Deal Practice	Mary Ann Jorgenson (Squires Sanders Dempsey,Labor Chair)	1
85.	Traditional Legal Matters on the Internet	Harrison Smith (Krooth & Altman LLP, Partner)	1

VENTURE CAPITAL/ENTREPRENEURSHIP

Chapter #	Title	Author	Units
123.	*Developing the Right Team Strategy	Sam Colella (Versant Ventures, Managing Director)	1
124.	*Successful Deal Doing	Patrick Ennis (ARCH Venture Partners, Partner)	1
125.	*Deal Making: The Interpersonal Aspects	John M. Abraham (Battery Ventures, Venture Partner)	1
126.	*The Art of Negotiations	Robert Chefitz (APAX Partners, General Partner)	1
127.	Future Opportunities	Michael Moritz (Sequoia Capital)	1
128.	*What VCs Look For	Heidi Roizen (SOFTBANK Venture Capital)	1
129.	International Opportunities	Jan Henric Buettner (Bertelsmann Ventures)	1
130.	The Importance of Technology	Alex Wilmerding (Boston Capital Ventures)	1
131.	Next Generation Success	Andrew Filipowski (divine interVentures)	1
132.	Internet Business Models	Suzanne King (New Enterprise Associates)	1
133.	Valuations and Key Indicators	Jonathan Goldstein (TA Associates)	1
134.	Early Stage Investing	Virginia Bonker (Blue Rock Capital)	1

* Denotes Best Selling Chapter

* Denotes Best Selling Chapter

Chapter #/Title	Author	Units
174. Technology Solutions to Business Needs	Michael S. Dunn (Encoda Systems, CTO, EVP)	1
175. Bridging Business and Technology	Mike Ragunas (StaplesDirect.com, CTO)	1
176. *The Art of Being a CTO - Fostering Change	Rick Bergquist (PeopleSoft, CTO)	1
178. Developing Best of Breed Technologies	Dr. David Whelan (Boeing, Space and Communications, CTO)	1
179. *Technology as a Strategic Weapon	Kevin Vasconi (Covisint, CTO)	1
180. Role of the CTO in a Venture-Backed Startup	Dan Burgin (Finali, CTO)	1
181. *Leading Technology During Turbulent Times	Frank Campagnoni (GE Global eXchange Services, CTO)	1
182. Staying on Top of Changing Technologies	Andrew Wolfe (SONICblue (formerly S3), CTO)	1
183. Building What the Market Needs	Neil Webber (Vignette, Former CTO, Co-Founder)	1
184. *Let the Business Dictate the Technology	Dwight Gibbs (The Motley Fool, Chief Techie Geek)	1
185. Technology Solutions: From the Ground Up	Peter Stern (Datek, CTO)	1
186. The Securities Behind Technology	Warwick Ford (VeriSign, CTO)	1
187. Building Leading Technology	Ron Moritz (Symantec, CTO)	1
188. The Business Sense Behind Technology	Dermot McCormack (Flooz.com, CTO and Co-Founder)	1
189. A Simple and Scaleable Technology Interface	Pavan Nigam (WebMD, Former CTO/Co-Fndr, Healtheon)	1
190. Designing the Right Technology Solution	Michael Wolfe (Kana Communications, VP, Engineering)	1
191. The Role of a CTO	Daniel Jaye (Engage, CTO and Co-Founder)	1
147. *Wireless Technology: Make It Simple	John Zeglis (AT&T Wireless, CEO)	1
148. *Bringing Value to the Consumer	Patrick McVeigh (OmniSky, Chairman and CEO)	1
149. Wireless Challenges	Sanjoy Malik (Air2Web, Founder, President and CEO)	1
150. The High Costs of Wireless	Paul Sethy (AirPrime, Founder & Chairman)	1

* Denotes Best Selling Chapter

Chapter #/Title	Author	Units
151. Developing Areas of Wireless	Reza Ahy (Aperto Networks, President & CEO)	1
152. *The Real Potential for Wireless	Martin Cooper (Arraycomm, Chairman & CEO)	1
153. Bringing Wireless into the Mainstream	Robert Gemmell (Digital Wireless, CEO)	1
154. VoiceXML	Alex Laats (Informio, CEO and Co-Founder)	1
155. Reaching the Epitome of Productivity	Rod Hoo (LGC Wireless, President and CEO)	1
156. Identifying Revenue Opportunities	Scott Bradner (Harvard Univ., Senior Technical Consultant)	1
157. The Wireless Satellite Space	Tom Moore (WildBlue, President and CEO)	1
158. *Memory Solutions for Semiconductor Industry	Steven R. Appleton (Micron Technology, Inc., CEO)	1
159. *Programmable Logic: The Digital Revolution	Wim Roelandts (Xilinx, Inc., CEO)	1
160. The Streaming Media Future	Jack Guedj, Ph.D. (Tvia, Inc., President)	1
161. Building a Winning Semiconductor Company	Igor Khandros, Ph.D. (FormFactor, Inc., President and CEO)	1
162. The Next Generation Silicon Lifestyle	Rajeev Madhavan (Magma, Chairman, CEO and President)	1
163. Semiconductors: The Promise of the Future	Steve Hanson (ON Semiconductor, President and CEO)	1
164. Dynamics of the Semiconductor Data Center	Eyal Waldman (Mellanox Technologies, LTD, CEO)	1
165. The Market-Driven Semiconductor Industry	Bob Lynch (Nitronex, President and CEO)	1
166. Semiconductors: Meeting Performance Demand	Satish Gupta (Cradle Technologies, President and CEO)	1
192. Balanced Internet Marketing Programs	Meg Brossy (Chief Marketing Officer, 24/7 Media)	1
193. Internet Ad Campaigns, Not Just Cool Ads	Brooke Correll (Wineshopper.com, VP Marketing)	1
194. Internet Advertising: Moving the Profit Needle	John Herr (Buy.com, Sr. VP Marketing & Advertising)	1
202. Future Internet Opportunities	Joe Krauss (Excite@Home, Founder)	1
203. Internet Future: An International Perspective	Charles Cohen (Beenz.com, CEO)	1

* Denotes Best Selling Chapter

Chapter #/Title	Author	Units
204. Valuing Internet Companies	John Segrich (CIBC, Internet Research Analyst)	1
205. The Potential for Personal Computing	Larry Cotter (Sandbox.com, CEO)	1
206. Using Innovation to Fulfill Customer Needs	Kyle Shannon (AGENCY.COM, Co-Founder)	1
207. Being a Leader in the Internet Economy	Jeff Sheahan (Egghead, CEO)	1
208. *Being a Sustainable Internet Business	Jonathan Nelson (Organic, Inc., CEO and Co-Founder)	1
209. Business-to-Business Effects on the Internet	Chris Vroom (Credit Suisse First Boston, Internet Analyst)	1
210. Risk & Uncertainty: Internet Co. Challenges	Joseph Howell (Emusic.com, Chief Financial Officer)	1
211. Focus on Profits in the Internet Economy	Lynn Atchison (Hoovers.com, Chief Financial Officer)	1
212. Cash Flow for Internet Companies	Tim Bixby (LivePerson, Chief Financial Officer)	1
213. Financial Accountability for Internet Companies	Greg Adams (Edgar Online, Chief Financial Officer)	1
214. Establishing Value for Internet Companies	Louis Kanganis (Nerve.com, Chief Financial Officer)	1
215. Managing Rapid Growth	David R. Henkel (Agillion.com, Chief Financial Officer)	1
216. Scalability and Profits for Internet Companies	Alan Breitman (Register.com, Chief Financial Officer)	1
217. *Building Real Value for Internet Companies	Joan Platt (CBS MarketWatch, Chief Financial Officer)	1
218. Financial Forecasting for the Internet Economy	David Gow (Ashford.com, Chief Financial Officer)	1
219. *Organizing the Internet Financial House	Mary Dridi (webMethods, Chief Financial Officer)	1
220. *Internet BizDev: Leveraging Your Value	John Somorjai (Keen.com, VP, Business Development)	1
221. Internet BizDev: Staying Focused	Todd Love (yesmail.com, Senior VP, Business Development)	1
222. Internet BizDev: Focusing on Corporate Goals	Chris Dobbrow (Real Names, SVP, Business Development)	1
223. Finding the Right Partners for an Internet Co.	Scott Wolf (NetCreations, SVP, Business Development)	1
224. Changing Internet Market Conditions	Daniel Conde (Imandi.com, Director, Business Development)	2

* Denotes Best Selling Chapter

Chapter #/Title	Author	Units
225. *Maximizing Time and Efficiencies	Bernie Dietz (WebCT, VP, Business Development)	1
226. Internet BizDev: Pushing the Right Buttons	Mark Bryant (LifeMinders.com, VP, Business Development)	1
227. BizDev Leadership in the Internet Economy	Robin Phelps (DigitalOwl.com, VP Business Development)	1
FINANCIAL		
244. *Merging Information Tech. & Accounting	Paul McDonald (Robert Half Int'l, Executive Director)	1
245. *The Accountant's Perspective	Gerald Burns (Moss Adams, Partner)	2
246. New Areas for Accountants	Dick Eisner (Richard A. Eisner & Co., Managing Partner)	1
247. *Audits & Analyzing Business Processes	Lawrence Rieger (Andersen, Global Managing Partner)	1
248. Accounting & the Entrepreneurial Market	Domenick Esposito (BDO Seidman, Vice Chairman)	1
250. E-Business Transformation	Fred Round (Ernst & Young, Director of eBusiness Tax)	1
251. Accounting: The UK/US Perspective	Colin Cook (KPMG, Head of Transaction Services - London)	1
252. The Changing Role of the Accountant	Jim McKerlie (Ran One, CEO)	1
253. The Future of Accounting	Harry Steinmetz (M.R. Weiser & Company, Partner)	1
INVESTING		
197. Who Wants to Become a Millionaire?	Laura Lee Wagner (American Express, Senior Advisor)	1
198. *The Gold is in Your Goals	Harry R. Tyler (Tyler Wealth Counselors, Inc., CEO)	1
199. *Timeless Tips for Building Your Nest Egg	Christopher P. Parr (Financial Advantage, Inc.)	1
200. It's What You Keep, Not Make, That Counts	Jerry Wade (Wade Financial Group, President)	1
201. Accumulating Your Million-Dollar Nest Egg	Marc Singer (Singer Xenos Wealth Management)	1
228. Time-Honored Investment Principles	Marilyn Bergen (CMC Advisors, LLC, Co-President)	1

* Denotes Best Selling Chapter

Chapter #/Title	Author	Units
229. *The Art & Science of Investing	Clark Blackman, II (Post Oak Capital Advisors, Managing Dir.)	1
240. Altering Investment Strategy for Retirement	Gary Mandell (The Mandell Group, President)	1
241. *Fair Value & Unfair Odds in Investing	Scott Opsal (Invista Capital Mngmt, Chief Investment Officer)	1
242. Earnings Count & Risk Hurts	Victoria Collins (Keller Group Investment Mngmnt, Principal)	1
243. *Navigating Turbulent Markets	Howard Weiss (Bank of America, Senior Vice President)	1
249. Building an All-Weather Personalized Portfolio	Sanford Axelroth & Robert Studin (First Financial Group)	1
254. Managing Your Wealth in Any Market	Gilda Borenstein (Merill Lynch, Wealth Mngmt. Advisor)	1
255. Winning Strategies for International Investing	Josephine Jiménez (Montgomery Asset Mngmnt, Principal)	1
256. The Psychology of a Successful Investor	Robert G. Morris (Lord Abbett, Dir. of Equity Investments)	1
257. *Investing for a Sustainable Future	Robert Allan Rikoon (Rikoon-Carret Investments, CEO)	1

OTHER

Chapter #/Title	Author	Units
258. *E-Health: The Adjustment of Internet Tech.	Robert A. Frist, Jr. (HealthStream, CEO and Chairman)	1
259. Health Care: The Paper Trail	Jonathan S. Bush (athenahealth, CEO and Chairman)	1
260. Consumer Backlash in the Health Care Industry	Peter W. Nauert (Ceres Group, CEO and Chairman)	1
261. Forging a Path in the New Health Care Industry	Dr. Norm Payson (Oxford Health, CEO & Chairman)	1
262. The Future of Clinical Trials	Dr. Paul Bleicher (Phase Forward, Chairman)	1
263. Health Care: Linking Everyone Together	John Holton (scheduling.com, CEO)	1
264. The Future of the Health Care Industry	Robert S. Cramer, Jr. (Adam.com, CEO and Chairman)	1
265. Being a Change Agent in Health Care	Kerry Hicks (HealthGrades, CEO & Chairman)	1
266. Personalized Solutions in Health Care	Dr. Mark Leavitt (Medscape, Chairman)	1

* Denotes Best Selling Chapter

THE FOCUSBOOK™

ASSEMBLE YOUR OWN BUSINESS BOOK™

Call Us Toll Free at 1-866-Aspatore (277-2867)
Or Tear Out the Next 2 Order Form Pages & Fax or Mail BOTH Pages To:
Aspatore Books, PO Box 883, Bedford, MA 01730
Or Fax To (617) 249-1970 (Preferred)

Name:

Email:

Shipping Address:

City: State: Zip:

Billing Address:

City: State: Zip:

Phone:

Book Content-5 Questions
1. What chapters would you like added? (Please list by number and author last name-i.e. 2-Jones.) (10 Units/Chapters is Standard for 1 Book.):

_____

_____

_____

_____

_____

_____

_____

2. If you are adding content, do you want it put at the beginning or end of the book? _____
3. Would you like the chapters in a particular order? (If this part is not filled out, we shall put them in random order.) If so, please list by author in order from first to last:

_____

_____

_____

_____

4. How would you like your name to read on the cover? (If you would like a company/university/course name added as well, please list it here with your name.): _____
5. What would you like the title of the book to be? (If none is added, we will simply put the information from the previous question.):

_____

To Order, Visit Us At <u>www.Aspatore.com</u> Or
Call Toll Free 1-866-Aspatore (277-2867)

Pricing-3 Steps

1. Quantity:

1 Book – $99   **2 Books** – $198 ($99 Per Book)
5 Books – $445 ($89 Per Book)**10 Books** – $790 ($79 Per Book)
50 Books – $2,450 ($49 Per Book) **100 Books** – $3,900 ($39 Per Book)
250 Books – $7,250 ($29 Per Book)   **500 Books** – $10,500 ($21 Per Book)
1000 Books – $15,000 ($15 Per Book) **5000 Books** – $49,750 ($9.95 Per
Book)

Number of Books: _____ *Price for Books:* _____

2. Decide the Number of Chapters in Your Book (If you are selecting only 10
units or less, please skip to No. 3-units are based on number of pages-most
chapters are 1 unit, however some are more depending on length.)

10 Units (Standard-Approximately 200-250 Pages) – No Extra Charge
15 Units – Please Add $25 Per Book if Ordering Between 1-10 Books, Add
$15 Per Book if Ordering 50-250 Books, Add $7.50 Per Book if Ordering 500-
5000 Books (So if ordering 50 books, the additional charge would be
50x10=$500)
25 Units – Please Add $75 Per Book if Ordering Between 1-10 Books, Add
$25 Per Book if Ordering 50-250 Books, Add $10 Per Book if Ordering 500-
5000 Books (So if ordering 50 books, the additional charge would be
50x25=$1,250)

Number of Units: _____ *Price for Additional Chapters:* _____

3. Adding Content (You must order at least 50 books to add content.) (If you
are not adding any content, skip this section.)

Adding 1 Page – Please Add $3 Per Book if Ordering 50-250 Books, Please
Add $2 Per Book if Ordering 500-5000 Books
Adding 2-9 Pages – Please Add $8 Per Book if Ordering 50-250 Books, Add
$4.00 Per Book if Ordering 500-5000 Books
Adding 10-49 Pages – Please Add $18 Per Book if Ordering 50-250 Books,
Add $9 Per Book if Ordering 500-5000 Books
Adding 50-99 Pages – Please Add $25 Per Book if Ordering 50-250 Books,
Add $13 Per Book if Ordering 500-5000 Books
Adding 100-149 Pages – Please Add $40 Per Book if Ordering 50-250 Books,
Add $20 Per Book if Ordering 500-5000 Books

(Please base page count by single spacing, 12 point font, Times New Roman
font type on 8.5X11 paper.) (Only charts and graphs that are smaller than 4
inches wide and 7 inches tall can be included.)
(A staff member will email you within 1 week of the order being placed to
coordinate receiving the materials electronically.)

Number of Pages Added: _____ *Price for Pages Added:* _____

To Order, Visit Us At www.Aspatore.com Or
Call Toll Free 1-866-Aspatore (277-2867)

PLEASE REPRINT THE FOLLOWING INFORMATION FROM THE PREVIOUS PAGE:

Number of Books: _____   ***Price for Books:*** _____
Number of Units: _____   ***Price for Additional Chapters:*** _____
Number of Pages Added: _____   ***Price for Pages Added:*** _____
    Total Price From Sections 1-3: _____

(If mailing in a check you can skip this section but please read fine print below and sign below-check must be received before a book is started-please email jennifer@aspatore.com for an alternate address if you are going to send the check via FedEx or UPS as the PO Box will not accept such shipments.)

Credit Card Type (Visa & Mastercard & Amex):

Credit Card Number:

Expiration Date:

Signature (Acceptance of Order and Terms & Conditions): _____

IF ADDING CONTENT, AFTER FAXING/MAILING THIS FORM, PLEASE EMAIL THE CONTENT AS A MICROSOFT WORD ATTACHMENT TO JENNIFER@ASPATORE.COM. THE EMAIL SHOULD INCLUDE YOUR NAME AND FOCUS BOOK NAME. YOU WILL RECEIVE AN EMAIL BACK WITHIN 24 HOURS IF THERE ARE ANY PROBLEMS/QUESTIONS FROM OUR STAFF.

*(Please note the billing address much match the address on file with your credit card company exactly)

For rush orders, guaranteed to ship within 1 week (for orders of 10 books or less) or within 2 weeks (for orders of 50 books or more) please initial here _____. An additional charge of $100 for orders of 10 or less books, $250 for orders of 11-25 books, $500 for orders of 25-100 books will be charged. If additional information is needed on rush orders, please email jennifer@aspatore.com.

If you would like your order sent via FedEx or UPS, for faster delivery, please enter your FedEx or UPS number here: _____ Please Circle One (FedEx/UPS). Delivery Type-Please Circle (Next Day, 2Day/Ground)

FOR QUESTIONS, PLEASE CONTACT ASPATORE BOOKS VIA EMAIL AT STORE@ASPATORE.COM.

Terms & Conditions - Prices include shipping and handling, unless a rush order is placed. All books are sent via media mail. We shall send a confirmation receipt to your email address. If ordering from Massachusetts, please add 5% sales tax on the order. If ordering from outside of the US, an additional $8.95 for shipping and handling costs will be charged for the first book, and $1.95 for each book thereafter. All books are paperback and will be shipped as soon as they become available. Sorry, no returns, refunds or cancellations at any point, even before the order has shipped or any additional content submitted. Aspatore Books is also not liable for any spacing errors in the book-only printing errors as determined by Aspatore Books. Any additions to the book will be formatted in relation to the rest of the text font size and type. Publication dates are subject to delay-please allow 1-4 weeks for delivery.

Please note that the rights to any content added to the Focusbook™ shall be retained by the author, and that Aspatore Books is simply printing the material in the Focusbook™, not publishing it. Aspatore Books shall not print, publish or distribute the content in any other media, or sell or distribute the content. The rights to all other material in the book shall remain the property of Aspatore Books and may not be reproduced or resold under any condition with out the express written consent of Aspatore Books. The author warrants and represents that to the best of his/her knowledge: (a) he/she has the right to print this material; (b) he/she has no contractual commitment of any kind which may prevent him/her from printing the material; (c) the contribution does not contain any unlawful, libelous or defamatory matter and does not infringe upon the rights, including copyright, of any other person or entity. The individual adding content to the Focusbook™ agrees to assume full liability for any content added to their FocusBook™, and agrees to indemnify and hold harmless Aspatore Books, its owners, officers, employees, agents, shareholders, parents, affiliates, subsidiaries, predecessors, agents, legal representatives, successors and assignees from and against any and all suits, claims, damages, liabilities, including attorneys' fees, based on or with respect to the falsity of any representation or warranty made to Aspatore Books, whether actual or claimed, or any infringement or related claims.

Inside the Minds: Chief Technology Officers-Developing,
Implementing and Capitalizing on the Best Technologies in the World
(ISBN: 1587620081)
Bigwig Briefs: Become a CTO-Leading CTOs Reveal How to Get
There, Stay There, and Empower Others That Work With You (ISBN:
1587620715)
Bigwig Briefs: Small Business Internet Advisor-Big Business Secrets
for Small Business Success on the Internet (ISBN: 1587620189)
Inside the Minds: Internet Marketing-Advertising, Marketing and
Building a Successful Brand on the Internet (ISBN: 1587620022)
Inside the Minds: Internet Bigwigs-Leading Internet CEOs and
Research Analysts Forecast the Future of the Internet Economy (ISBN:
1587620103)
Inside the Minds: Internet CFOs-Information Every Individual Should
Know About the Financial Side of Internet Companies (ISBN: 158762)
Inside the Minds: Internet BizDev-The Golden Rules to Inking Deals in
the Internet Industry (ISBN: 1587620057)
Bigwig Briefs: The Golden Rules of the Internet Economy-The Future
of the Internet Economy (Even After the Shakedown) (ISBN:
1587620138)
Inside the Minds: Internet Lawyers-Important Answers to Issues For
Every Entrepreneur, Lawyer & Anyone With a Web Site (ISBN:
1587620065)

LAW

Inside the Minds: Leading Labor Lawyers-Labor Chairs Reveal the
Secrets to the Art & Science of Labor Law (ISBN: 1587621614)
Inside the Minds: Leading Litigators-Litigation Chairs Revel the
Secrets to the Art & Science of Litigation (ISBN: 1587621592)
Inside the Minds: Leading IP Lawyers-IP Chairs Reveal the Secrets to
the Art & Science of IP Law (ISBN: 1587621606)
Inside the Minds: Leading Deal Makers-Negotiations, Leveraging Your
Position and the Art of Deal Making (ISBN: 1587620588)
Inside the Minds: Internet Lawyers-Important Answers to Issues For
Every Entrepreneur, Lawyer & Anyone With a Web Site (ISBN:
1587620065)
Bigwig Briefs: The Art of Deal Making-The Secrets to the Deal Making
Process (ISBN: 1587621002)

Bigwig Briefs: Career Options for Law School Students-Leading Partners Reveal the Secrets to Choosing the Best Career Path (ISBN: 1587621010)

MARKETING/ADVERTISING/PR

Inside the Minds: Leading Marketers-Leading Chief Marketing Officers Reveal the Secrets to Building a Billion Dollar Brand (ISBN: 1587620537)

Inside the Minds: Leading Advertisers-Advertising CEOs Reveal the Tricks of the Advertising Profession (ISBN: 1587620545)

Inside the Minds: The Art of PR-Leading PR CEOs Reveal the Secrets to the Public Relations Profession (ISBN: 1587620634)

Inside the Minds: PR Visionaries-The Golden Rules of PR and Becoming a Senior Level Advisor With Your Clients (ISBN: 1587621517)

Inside the Minds: Internet Marketing-Advertising, Marketing and Building a Successful Brand on the Internet (ISBN: 1587620022)

Bigwig Briefs: Online Advertising-Successful and Profitable Online Advertising Programs (ISBN: 1587620162)

Bigwig Briefs: Guerrilla Marketing -The Best of Guerrilla Marketing-Big Marketing Ideas For a Small Budget (ISBN: 1587620677)

Bigwig Briefs: Become a VP of Marketing-How to Get There, Stay There, and Empower Others That Work With You (ISBN: 1587620707)

FINANCIAL

Inside the Minds: Leading Accountants-The Golden Rules of Accounting & the Future of the Accounting Industry and Profession (ISBN: 1587620529)

Inside the Minds: Internet CFOs-Information Every Individual Should Know About the Financial Side of Internet Companies (ISBN: 1587620057)

Inside the Minds: The Financial Services Industry-The Future of the Financial Services Industry & Professions (ISBN: 1587620626)

Inside the Minds: Leading Investment Bankers-Leading I-Bankers Reveal the Secrets to the Art & Science of Investment Banking (ISBN: 1587620618)

Bigwig Briefs: Become a CFO-Leading CFOs Reveal How to Get There, Stay There, and Empower Others That Work With You (ISBN: 1587620731)

Bigwig Briefs: Become a VP of Biz Dev-How to Get There, Stay There, and Empower Others That Work With You (ISBN: 1587620723)
Bigwig Briefs: Career Options for MBAs-I-Bankers, Consultants & CEOs Reveal the Secrets to Choosing the Best Career Path (ISBN: 1587621029)

INVESTING

Inside the Minds: Building a $1,000,000 Nest Egg -Simple, Proven Ways for Anyone to Build a $1M Nest Egg On Your Own Terms (ISBN: 1587622157)
Inside the Minds: Leading Wall St. Investors -The Best Investors of Wall Street Reveal the Secrets to Profiting in Any Economy (ISBN: 1587621142)

OTHER

Inside the Minds: The New Health Care Industry-The Future of the Technology Charged Health Care Industry (ISBN: 1587620219)
Inside the Minds: The Real Estate Industry-The Future of Real Estate and Where the Opportunities Will Lie (ISBN: 1587620642)
Inside the Minds: The Telecommunications Industry-Telecommunications Today, Tomorrow and in 2030 (ISBN: 1587620669)
Inside the Minds: The Automotive Industry-Leading CEOs Share Their Knowledge on the Future of the Automotive Industry (ISBN: 1587620650)

ASPATORE

Executive Business Intelligence